Second Edition

Rediscovering
an EVANGELICAL
HERITAGE

A Tradition and Trajectory *of* Integrating
Piety and Justice

DONALD W. DAYTON
with DOUGLAS M. STRONG

Foreword by Jim Wallis

Baker Academic
a division of Baker Publishing Group
Grand Rapids, Michigan

Published by Baker Academic
a division of Baker Publishing Group
P.O. Box 6287, Grand Rapids, MI 49516-6287
www.bakeracademic.com

Printed in the United States of America

Library of Congress Cataloging-in-Publication Data is on file at the Library of Congress, Washington, DC.

ISBN 978-0-8010-4961-3

Unless otherwise indicated, Scripture quotations are from the King James Version of the Bible.

Scripture quotations labeled NRSV are from the New Revised Standard Version of the Bible, copyright © 1989, by the Division of Christian Education of the National Council of the Churches of Christ in the United States of America. Used by permission. All rights reserved.

Illustration credits by page number: **35**: *Post American*, now *Sojourners Magazine*, (800)-714-7474, www.sojo.net; **54**: Cover of the *Post American*, now *Sojourners Magazine*, (800)-714-7474, www.sojo.net; **62**: Charles G. Finney, *Lectures on Systematic Theology* . . . (London: William Tegg & Co., 1851), frontispiece; **76**: Wendell Phillips Garrison and Francis Jackson Garrison, *William Lloyd Garrison, 1805–1879: The Story of His Life Told by His Children*, vol. 2, 1835–1840 (New York: The Century Co., 1885), between pp. 116 and 117; **90**: General Catalogue of Oberlin College, 1833–1908 (Oberlin, OH: Oberlin College, 1909); **100**: James H. Fairchild, *Oberlin: The Colony and the College, 1833–1883* (Oberlin, OH: E. J. Goodrich, 1883), between pp. 126 and 127; **103**: Laura S. Haviland, *A Woman's Life-Work: Including Thirty Years' Service on the Underground Railroad and in the War*, 5th ed. (Grand Rapids, MI: S. B. Shaw, Publisher, © 1881), 292; **104**: Samuel Ringgold Ward, *Autobiography of a Fugitive Negro* (London: John Snow, 1855), frontispiece; **114**: Julia Griffiths, ed., *Autographs for Freedom*, 2nd series (Auburn, NY: Alden, Beardsley & Co.; Rochester, NY: Wanzer, Beardsley, & Co., 1854), between pp. 162 and 163; **126**: Ira Ford McLeister, *History of the Wesleyan Methodist Church of America* (Syracuse, NY: Wesleyan Methodist Pub. Association, 1934), plate five, between pp. 26 and 27; **145**: Frederick St. George De Lautour Booth-Tucker, *The Life of Catherine Booth, the Mother of the Salvation Army*, vol. 1 (Revell, 1892), frontispiece; **146**: Richard Wheatley, *Life and Letters of Mrs. Phoebe Palmer* (New York: W. C. Palmer, Publisher, 1881 [1876]), frontispiece; **147**: Amanda Smith, *An Autobiography: The Story of the Lord's Dealings with Mrs. Amanda Smith, the Colored Evangelist* (Chicago: Meyer & Brother, Publishers, 1893), frontispiece; **155**: *Earnest Christian* 9 (1865), frontispiece; **157**: E. A. Girvin, *Phineas F. Bresee: A Prince in Israel: A Biography* (Kansas City, MO: Pentecostal Nazarene Publishing House, 1916), frontispiece.

14 15 16 17 18 19 20   7 6 5 4 3 2 1

Contents

Acknowledgment

Thanks to the editors of *Post American* (now *Sojourners*) for permission to use material that first appeared in their pages in different form as a ten-part series titled "Recovering a Heritage," published from June–July 1974 through May 1975.

A Note about
Editions of This Book

As of 2014, there are three extant versions of this book. The first edition, titled *Discovering an Evangelical Heritage*, was published by Harper & Row in 1976. A reprint of that edition, under the same name, and unaltered except for the addition of a new preface by the author, Donald Dayton, was published by Hendrickson in 1988. This current publication, the second edition, has the slightly altered name of *Rediscovering an Evangelical Tradition*. In addition to the original text by Donald Dayton, which has been lightly edited, this second edition includes a new introduction, conclusion, and five chapter postscripts written by Douglas Strong, along with fresh illustrations and a new foreword by Jim Wallis. The second edition was published by Baker Academic in 2014.

Foreword

By Jim Wallis

When Don Dayton wrote a series of essays titled "Recovering a Heritage" for *Sojourners* magazine (then called *Post American*), he was responding to a young evangelical movement that at the time seemed radical, but was in fact a return to an orthodoxy that had been lost. These essays eventually became his seminal book, *Discovering an Evangelical Heritage*. In it Dayton masterfully recounted the work of revivalist minister Charles G. Finney, reformists Theodore Weld and the Grimke sisters, and the men and women of Oberlin Colony, and he reminded readers of the history of the evangelical movement in America as a call back to our best spiritual values. I had never heard about an evangelical movement that was once committed to social justice and even helped to change America in its time.

In *Discovering an Evangelical Heritage* Dayton showed that many evangelical Christians in the nineteenth century didn't distinguish between a private faith focused exclusively on personal salvation and radical concern for the poor and oppressed. Personal piety was largely connected to works that went beyond charity to social reform and justice. It wasn't an evangelical faith concerned only about heaven and the life hereafter but about bringing the kingdom of God into *this world*. As a result, evangelicals were heavily involved in the abolition of slavery, fighting for the poor, and women's rights. Evangelical revivals called people not only to personal atonement but to putting faith into action. At their "altar calls" people would come to Christ and immediately sign up for the anti-slavery campaign!

Since its founding, *Sojourners* has articulated the biblical call to social justice. For many of us who grew up in the post-war evangelical American churches where faith had been privatized, Don Dayton helped us understand that our longing to embrace the world was grounded in both Scripture and history. He revealed the public evangelical faith that is our great inheritance. And that revelation even helped to renew our faith personally. Dayton's voice in our magazine was a dramatic historical demonstration that our evangelical heritage involved a deeply personal faith that expressed itself in a commitment to real change—not just in our hearts but in the world that God so loved. The kingdom of God is the central message of the New Testament, intended to change the world and us with it.

In *Rediscovering an Evangelical Heritage,* an expansion of the original book, Don Dayton and Doug Strong show it is not heretical or "communist" to talk about social justice in the church. On the contrary, a personal faith that issues itself in a fundamental commitment to social justice is the very stuff of orthodoxy and is deeply embedded in American history. Dayton showed us young sojourners that we weren't the first people to connect faith to justice, but that integrating both goes back into the heart of church history. Separating personal faith from public expression is a rather recent American "heresy." That was humbling, reassuring, and grounding for us as well.

The good news now is that a new generation of evangelical Christians is hungry to do exactly what these earlier reformers were doing. So I would urge you to read this update of a classic book, and ask how we can put our evangelical faith into action that makes its own history.

Jim Wallis
July 2014

Introduction to the
Second Edition (2014)

A Tradition of Integrated Faith

By Douglas M. Strong

Three incidents illustrate the relevance of this book's message—a relevance that comes from its forty-year reputation of drawing attention to an overlooked interpretation of the evangelical movement and from its enduring capacity to offer a historical foundation for the hopes and longings of American Christians. The first incident comes from 1844; the second from 1975; and the third from a week ago.

In the 1840s, Robert Baird, a Pennsylvanian residing in Switzerland, wrote the earliest comprehensive text describing American religion. Baird published his pioneering work in two places: Glasgow and New York. The Scottish edition assisted the British and Europeans to grasp the seemingly odd faith perspectives of their cousins across the ocean, while the American edition helped Baird's countrymen and women understand and interpret their own religious milieu. In the verbose style typical of the era, Baird's title—*Religion in America: Or, An Account of the Origin, Relation to the State, and Present Condition of the Evangelical Churches in the United States; with Notices of the Unevangelical Denominations*—revealed one of the central arguments of his writing: according to Baird, American churches could be described most clearly by a category he called "evangelical." The 1844 printing of Baird's book, then, provides a convenient chronological point identifying when most nineteenth-century American Christians perceived themselves collectively as evangelicals.

Baird did not coin the term "evangelical." It had been used since the sixteenth century to refer to Lutherans in Germany and since the eighteenth century to describe the pietistic religious renewal that occurred among English-speaking Protestants. In *Religion in America*, Baird asserted that evangelicalism had become the normative faith expression in the United States. He admitted that "unevangelical" denominations existed in America, a catchall designation for such unlikely bedfellows as Catholics, Unitarians, Universalists, Shakers, and Mormons. But in Baird's mind, these unevangelical groups were out of step with the overall American religious spirit because they "oppose religious revivals." It was evangelicals, he suggested, who were the true paragons of Christianity in the United States.[1]

What commonalities did Baird find among the wide range of churches he identified as evangelical—various kinds of Presbyterians, various kinds of Methodists (including both predominantly white and African American Methodist denominations), various kinds of Baptists (white and black), Congregationalists, Lutherans, two-thirds of the Episcopalians, some Friends (Quakers), various Anabaptists, and many of those from ethnically based Reformed churches? The primary mark of unity Baird found was that evangelicals in the United States participated in "revivals of religion" so that every American could be spiritually transformed. Baird also determined that, in the United

1. Robert Baird, *Religion in America: Or, An Account of the Origin, Relation to the State, and Present Condition of the Evangelical Churches in the United States; with Notices of the Unevangelical Denominations* (New York: Harper and Brothers, 1844), 612–57. While Baird's categorizing of denominations into "evangelical" and "unevangelical" groups, one of which he considered normative and the other not normative, would be viewed by many today as unacceptable, most nineteenth-century Protestants held such a view. See Robert Handy, *A Christian America: Protestant Hopes and Historical Realities* (New York: Oxford University Press, 1984), 24–29.

States, evangelicals were unified due to the fact that they upheld the democratic "voluntary system" of support for churches, as opposed to being state-supported. Christianity prospered under voluntarism, Baird contended, and one of the most noticeable results of this religious freedom was that revivals had become "a consistent part of the religious system of our country."

The major characteristic that drew these varied Protestants together, then, was not a shared belief in a common dogmatic system since the diverse churches he described disagreed strongly about many of their cherished tenets, such as predestination, Christian perfection, believer's baptism, and the correct understanding of church polity. Neither did Baird assume that they all affirmed a precise view regarding the nature of Christian Scripture; in fact, Baird said almost nothing about the Bible except that evangelical faith was based on its teachings. Rather, what American evangelicals shared was a "vital piety" expressed through revivalism—a revivalism that flourished due to the disestablished nature of the American churches. Baird observed a mutual commitment among evangelicals to encourage every individual to experience a "new birth"—an imminent, transformative, volitional encounter with Jesus Christ. "Nineteen-twentieths of all the evangelical churches in [the United States] believe that there is such a thing as 'being born again,' 'born of the Spirit.'" Evangelicals, Baird wrote, avowed an empirical "feeling of the supernatural," a "sense of the peculiar presence of God, the sanctifying Spirit." "The great body of evangelical Christians," he declared, "nearly all agree" on the need for a "change of heart" by "the direct interposition of God," resulting in "immediate right action" because "God requires them to become instantly holy."[2]

None of the evangelical churches Baird described would have denied the importance of orthodox belief derived from Scripture. However,

---

2. Baird, *Religion in America*, xiii, 196–217, 220, 267, 269, 270, 287, 414–15, 505–6, 658–64. While not asserting a unified dogmatic system, Baird nonetheless assumed that evangelical churches jointly held to a generic sense of Protestant orthodoxy, which he referred to as "soundness of doctrine." But he spends only one paragraph of his seven-hundred-page book listing the beliefs that he determined were commonly held: the nature of the Trinity, human depravity, the divinity and atoning work of Christ, the necessity of regeneration, and a final judgment. "On these doctrines . . . there is no difference among the evangelical churches" (414).

American evangelicals in 1844 were not held together primarily by their affirmation of correct doctrine coming from a perfect Bible as much as by their commitment to a sanctified life coming from a personal Jesus. Baird's interpretation of American religion as being generally evangelical, and his perspective that the main characteristic of evangelical churches was a consensus regarding the need for a decisive, affective conversion to Christ to be followed by holy living, became the dominant understanding of American religious historiography throughout the nineteenth century and into the early twentieth century.

But by the 1920s, interpreters of American religion recognized that Baird's broad, experientially based evangelicalism had divided into at least two streams, often referred to as modernism/liberalism and fundamentalism/conservatism. The fundamentalist strain arose primarily from the disputations of Princeton Seminary and the eschatological teachings of dispensational Bible conferences, both of which were reacting against modernist preaching and theology. This fundamentalist voice grew increasingly shrill and culture-denigrating as its influence within American society waned during the early decades of the twentieth century.[3]

By the post–World War II era, some younger fundamentalists wished to move away from the societally antagonistic attitudes of their parents, and reappropriated the term "evangelicalism" for themselves. While more open to the larger culture than their immediate predecessors, these post-fundamentalist evangelicals[4] (or, perhaps more properly, "neo-evangelicals") still felt a strong need to extend the battle against the perceived errors of Protestant liberalism. To be sure, mid-century liberal theologians and mainline church leaders did, in fact, espouse a number of problematic ideas worth critiquing. Nonetheless, many of those in the mid- to late twentieth century who took on the name "evangelical" tended to articulate their beliefs in a particularly reactive

3. See Douglas M. Strong, *They Walked in the Spirit: Personal Faith and Social Action in America* (Louisville: Westminster John Knox, 1998), xxiii–xxxi.

4. By referring to neo-evangelicals as "post-fundamentalist," I do not mean to imply that they abandoned fundamentalist doctrinal emphases; rather, they sought to modify and smooth out the sharp edges of fundamentalist rhetoric while generally retaining "orthodox" (fundamental) beliefs.

mode. Rather than challenging liberalism's theological innovations by reasserting classic Christian affirmations regarding Jesus's saving action on the cross and the final victory of God's power over sin, neo-evangelicals instead promulgated strict formulations of biblical inerrancy, narrowly defined neo-Reformed or premillennialist doctrines, and extraneous defenses of the "American way of life." Indeed, some post-fundamentalists stressed that fidelity to these propositional distinctives and nationalistic views was more indicative of faithful evangelicalism than the older revivalistic understanding—as written about by Baird in 1844 and then commonly used throughout the nineteenth century—that genuine evangelicalism could be identified most clearly by a born-again experience of God's grace resulting in ethical action.[5]

The second illustrative event took place in the mid-1970s, while I was an undergraduate at Houghton College, a small, well-respected Wesleyan Methodist institution located in western New York State. I was deeply grateful for the piety represented at the college, which encouraged students to develop a fervent and abiding relationship with a personal, interactive God. However, during my time there, I became increasingly disturbed—as did a number of my classmates—with the apolitical or even regressive social views promoted by some self-described evangelicals, especially regarding issues of race relations, gender roles, and the need to alleviate poverty. These neo-evangelicals did not see any need to confront the existing state of affairs in the country. But to us, such nonactivist attitudes seemed incongruent with the values of a Savior who, according to the New Testament, challenged social structures, broke down ethnic and gender stereotypes, preached to the poor, and lifted up the marginalized.

5. In a famous tract titled *The Four Spiritual Laws*, created in 1952 by the post-fundamentalist, neo-evangelical Bill Bright, "faith" is dependent on the "facts" of the Bible, with "feeling" coming far behind both faith and facts. Indeed, according to Bright's tract (p. 12), Christians "do not depend upon feelings," since trust in God can occur without any affective appropriation of faith. Bright's mid-twentieth-century articulation of belief tied primarily to propositional orthodoxy can be contrasted to the view of the seventeenth- and eighteenth-century Pietists, such as John Wesley, and most nineteenth-century evangelicals, who—though maintaining the importance of sound doctrine—also held that an assurance of faith via properly ordered "Christian affections" and the "witness of the Spirit," resulting in sanctified living, is what is most necessary for believers. See Wesley's two sermons titled *The Witness of the Spirit*.

In the spring of 1975, Donald W. Dayton, the son of the college's president and himself a graduate of the college, came as a guest lecturer. Dayton's visit provided a hopeful vision because his lectures (some of which subsequently made their way into the first edition of this book a year later) offered example after example of nineteenth-century evangelicals—including the founders of the college—who embodied a New Testament–shaped combination of devotional enthusiasm and social justice advocacy. This integrated spirituality stirred our hearts to action and motivated us to be thoughtful, socially conscious evangelicals. In contrast to the post-fundamentalist, neo-evangelical preoccupation with doctrinal purity, biblical literalism, and anti-Communism, Dayton highlighted a different sort of evangelicalism by unearthing and championing the stories of the revival-oriented evangelicals whom Baird had lifted up back in 1844. Dayton's narrative of socially active Christians contradicted the negative reputation of revivalism as an otherworldly enterprise concerned only with saving souls. Dayton's *Discovering an Evangelical Heritage* became a go-to resource for a whole cadre of folks in the 1970s who were seeking to cultivate personal faith experiences and simultaneously live out what we perceived to be the mandates of an ethic grounded in the narrative of the Bible we were reading.

The third incident comes from a week ago. When speaking with my twentysomething son about the republication of this book, he stated bluntly: "We've got to drop the 'evangelical' label. My friends and I don't want to be referred to that way because it carries such baggage." This is from a young man who, by any objective standard, would be characterized as the epitome of a millennial-generation evangelical—a proud alumnus of an esteemed Christian college, a member of the audio visual crew at a regionally well-known megachurch, and an eager employee of a start-up video production firm founded by an entrepreneurial Christian businessman. Because he's concerned about the way evangelicalism is being perceived by the larger culture, he's not impressed by the fact that his college or his parents or his church have long been connected with this movement.

A 2012 article in the *New York Times* described the lack of interest among younger evangelicals in their religious heritage. Why is that? Richard Flory of the Center for Religion and Civic Culture at the

University of Southern California responded in a letter to the editor that "if Jerry Falwell, James Dobson, and the forefathers of the evangelical right have done anything for evangelicals, they have made large segments of a generation embarrassed to call themselves evangelicals, leading many to head out the church doors." Not all of these young men and women have left the church, but many are disillusioned with what they perceive of evangelicalism. Even so, Flory's research found that contemporary Christians still seek faith communities where they can know God, be known by others, and serve one another and the broader community. "If evangelicalism is to have a future, it must examine why younger people are leaving and construct congregations and ministries within which they can be active participants."[6]

This book is the story of nineteenth-century evangelicals who established precisely that type of faith community. By their example, these predecessors provide a model for a different breed of evangelical—a breed Dayton raised up in the 1970s and who can now be a model for a new generation of emerging adults. This current generation may not be persuaded to adopt again the moniker "evangelical," due to the negative sociopolitical caricature of the term portrayed in American popular culture, but they may nonetheless be evangelically minded—in the pietistic sense—for they too want to live out an ethos of scripturally grounded, spiritually passionate, socially active Christian faith.[7]

The conviction that an integrated evangelical tradition still has currency and, indeed, can offer a way forward for twenty-first-century Christians is what motivates the publication of a new edition of this book. The book's 2014 reissue highlights three distinct periods of American church history, as represented by the three incidents related above. First, Donald Dayton's original chapters (which follow this newly written introduction) chronicle a half century or so in the nineteenth century when self-described evangelicals (of the Robert Baird revivalistic variety, not the post-fundamentalist variety) provided a powerful witness

6. Richard Flory, "Disaffection among Young Evangelicals," letter to the editor in response to "The Decline of Evangelical America" (December 16, 2012), *New York Times*, December 21, 2012.

7. David Kinnaman, with Aly Hawkins, *You Lost Me: Why Young Christians Are Leaving the Church . . . and Rethinking Faith* (Grand Rapids: Baker Books, 2011), 12, 77.

of spiritually enlivened Christians engaged in biblically prompted social change. In this second edition (2014), new "postscripts" have been added to many of the original chapters, in order to provide further insight on the various subjects and to highlight their relevance.

Second, the original occasion for the writing of Dayton's chapters was a series of articles that he published in *Post American* (later renamed *Sojourners*),[8] a 1970s alternative Christian magazine, and then collated into the book. (Dayton also presented some of the chapters as lectures, such as the ones I heard at Houghton College during the same period.) The reception this book received at the time reveals much about the era in which it was published, particularly since it became an iconic text among the younger Christians of that era, and especially for "progressive evangelical" leaders such as Jim Wallis, the founder of the Sojourners community. *Discovering an Evangelical Heritage* represented a moment in time, in the aftermath of the turbulent 1960s, when Christians sought to reclaim this heritage for the challenges of a new day. The book, then, is both a secondary and a primary source from two eras—the nineteenth century and the post-Vietnam/Watergate period of the twentieth century.

Third, in the midst of a new generation brought up in the twenty-first century, American Christians currently find themselves in a very different cultural context religiously, where liberal, mainline Christianity is in serious decline and disarray; conservative, neo-evangelical Christianity, which had become dominant, has stagnated (except among immigrant groups); and established religion in all forms is on the defensive. Yet, still, there is a desire, especially among young adults, for a form of scripturally based Christianity in which social justice is perceived as the natural outworking of deep faith[9]—an evangelicalism much like the one Dayton discovered from the 1800s, uncovered for the 1970s, and that can be rediscovered again for today.[10]

8. The magazine's title was variously presented as *The Post-American* or *Post American*. Later, the name changed to *Sojourners*.

9. For more insight, see "Three Spiritual Journeys of Millennials," *Barna Group*, May 9, 2013, https://www.barna.org/barna-update/teens-nextgen/612-three-spiritual-journeys-of-millennials.

10. One of Dayton's original ideas for a title for this book was "Rediscovering an Evangelical Heritage," but that idea was rejected by Harper & Row's editors. By using

The Dayton Thesis—Articulated and Critiqued

While Dayton did not refer to Baird's *Religion in America*, his interpretative perspective in *Discovering an Evangelical Heritage* corresponded with Baird's premise that conversionistic, affective faith was the major expression of nineteenth-century Christianity. Dayton described the historical context of this experiential faith more definitively than Baird, by stating that "when American church historians use the term 'evangelical,' they generally refer to the emergence of the Arminian, pietistic revivalism that was epitomized in [Charles G.] Finney." Dayton then went even further by spotlighting those particular nineteenth-century evangelicals who worked for social change.

This was Dayton's specific contribution to American religious historiography: popularizing and making accessible a tradition of evangelical social activism.[11] In his original chapters, Dayton brought to life a nexus of pastors, evangelists, educators, businesspeople, reformers, colleges, seminaries, voluntary societies, mission organizations, and split-away denominations who were galvanized by their evangelical faith to advocate for the transformation of American society. Their awakened social conscience created ferment for more than a generation through the auspices of "New School" Presbyterian and Congregationalist revivals, Methodist camp meetings, city missions, the Holiness movement, and (discussed in Dayton's later writings) early Pentecostalism. From the 1830s through the 1890s, Dayton demonstrated, evangelicals led the charge in social movements to abolish slavery, to advance the rights of women, to advocate for the poor, to urge the temperate use of alcohol in order to stem degradation and domestic abuse, to resist the commercialization of society, and to work against urban blight. Rather than being isolated or idiosyncratic

the term "rediscovering" in this edition, we hearken back to Dayton's first inclinations while also emphasizing the renewed relevance of the book.

11. Whitney L. Cross, *The Burned-Over District* (Ithaca, NY: Cornell University Press, 1950); Charles Cole, *The Social Ideas of the Northern Evangelists* (New York: Columbia University Press, 1954); and Timothy L. Smith, *Revivalism and Social Reform in Mid-Nineteenth Century America* (New York: Abingdon, 1956), were precursors to Dayton, but the publication of Dayton's book with Harper & Row resulted in influencing a broader general audience, two decades after the earlier monographs.

instances of the integration of a social and personal gospel, Dayton's case studies compellingly showed that there is (in Dayton's words) "a great heritage of Evangelical social witness."

Indeed, this social-reform heritage represented the natural fruit of evangelical piety while the now-dominant post-fundamentalist forms of (neo-)evangelicalism represent a deflection from (and perhaps a hijacking of) authentic evangelical identity. Dayton acknowledged that traditions and preachers who opposed revival-generated social reforms were part of the religious movement referred to as evangelicalism, but he contended that those church bodies "were not at the heart of American evangelical experience." As Dayton writes: "In the nineteenth century, Finney's 'New School' Presbyterian views dominated evangelicalism, but the twentieth century has seen the increasing impact of the 'Old School' Princeton Theology. This shift is widely discernible in evangelicalism. . . . The significance of such developments for evangelical social reform is that the Princeton Theology incarnated extremely conservative social views." For Dayton and those who have followed in his line of thought, rather than accepting the usual depiction (in the press, for instance) of the word "evangelical" as synonymous with the word "conservative," these terms ought instead to be perceived as oxymoronic. Yet many in the major media continue to overidentify evangelicalism (as a religious movement) with conservatism (as a political movement).[12]

Why is there such a pervasive perception that evangelicals are, and always have been, conservatives—not just theologically, but also socially and politically? The problem, Dayton asserted, in his tenth chapter, titled "Whatever Happened to Evangelicalism?," is that the integrated heritage of socially active piety "was buried and largely forgotten" by the 1950s and '60s. Dayton states that this historical amnesia occurred due to several factors: a routinization and institutionalization process common among dynamic movements diluted the reform impulse; the challenge of complex social realities and entrenched systems of power deflated the reformers' hopes for social change; a shift occurred among

12. See Steve Wilkens and Don Thorsen, *Everything You Know About Evangelicals Is Wrong (Well, Almost Everything)* (Grand Rapids: Baker Books, 2010).

evangelicals from an optimistic postmillennial eschatology to a fatalistic premillennial end-times perspective (expecting the imminent return of Christ without the transformation of society); and the promulgation of Protestant scholasticism created a pessimistic worldview resulting in a "great reversal" regarding the need for Christians to work for social change.[13]

Both Dayton's depiction of socially engaged, faith-based reform in the nineteenth century and his narrative of the decline of that impetus by the mid-twentieth century struck a chord with many 1970s Christian activists, who instinctively understood both the promise and the precariousness of a movement for evangelical social action. Jim Wallis, for instance, regularly described himself as a "nineteenth-century evangelical." In addition to the young, evangelical social reformers who grabbed onto this narrative as their own, a host of historians and theologians also adopted and then furthered Dayton's argument—some explicitly and others more indirectly. For a popular book derived from serialized articles—never intending to be a scholarly monograph—*Discovering an Evangelical Heritage* nevertheless had quite an influence on the academic community. Dayton's own scholarly trajectory also built on the themes he first developed in this book: particularly the definition and usefulness of evangelicalism as a category; the deleterious effect of upward mobility on religious movements for social change; and the implicit radicalism of the nascent Holiness and Pentecostal movements.[14]

But not all scholars agreed with Dayton. As with any bold thesis, some proffered alternative views; in this case, the scholarly challenge

13. The term "great reversal" was coined by Timothy L. Smith in *Revivalism and Social Reform*, and then picked up by David O. Moberg in *The Great Reversal: Evangelism Versus Social Concern* (Philadelphia: J. B. Lippincott, 1972).

14. See Donald W. Dayton, "Some Doubts about the Usefulness of the Category 'Evangelical,'" in *The Variety of American Evangelicalism*, ed. Donald W. Dayton and Robert K. Johnston (Knoxville: University of Tennessee Press, 1991), 245–51; Dayton, "'Good News for the Poor': The Wesleyan Experience after Wesley," in *The Portion of the Poor: The Good News to the Poor in the Wesleyan Tradition*, ed. M. Douglas Meeks (Nashville: Abingdon, 1995); Dayton, "Yet Another Layer of the Onion, or Opening the Ecumenical Door to Let the Riffraff In," *Ecumenical Review* 40, no. 1 (1988): 87–110; Dayton, *Theological Roots of Pentecostalism* (Metuchen, NJ: Scarecrow, 1987).

came from two directions—the right and the left. Not surprisingly, the first pushback originated from the post-fundamentalist, neo-evangelical establishment. Indeed, even before Dayton's book focused new attention on the role of Charles Finney, the famous nineteenth-century revivalist's reputation as a positive exemplar of evangelical faith had been questioned by a certain strand of conservative historians and theologians such as J. Edwin Orr, Richard Lovelace, and John Gerstner. Gerstner, for example, called Finney "the greatest foe of nineteenth century Evangelicalism," due to Finney's New School theology. Presumably, for Gerstner, only a certain type of Old School Presbyterian could count as truly evangelical. Others dismissed the evangelical orthodoxy of Finney and anyone who deviated theologically from a very particular kind of conservative Calvinism.[15]

A more substantive and specific challenge to Dayton's argument appeared the year after the publication of *Discovering an Evangelical Heritage*, when a debate ensued in print between Dayton and religious historian George Marsden. In a review essay, Marsden contended that Dayton overextended his case when he claimed that Finney, Jonathan Blanchard, Luther Lee, and the Tappan brothers represented the mainstream nineteenth-century evangelical current. Marsden declared that Dayton's argument that "radical reform was a trait of most of those near the center of nineteenth-century evangelicalism" was wishful thinking. Marsden countered that Finney's ideas were not accepted widely and that other nonrevivalistic traditions were more prototypical of evangelicalism. Marsden stated that most evangelicals, and even most Methodists, took socially conservative stances and did not tout social reforms. He charged that Dayton ignored the widespread conservative leanings of the evangelical movement, especially in the political arena. Marsden also asserted that Dayton neglected the fact that the primary means by which the revivalists lived out their commitment to the poor and oppressed was through

15. John H. Gerstner, "The Theological Boundaries of Evangelical Faith," in *The Evangelicals: What They Believe, Who They Are, Where They Are Changing*, ed. David F. Wells and John D. Woodbridge (Nashville: Abingdon, 1975), 27; Richard F. Lovelace, *Dynamics of Spiritual Life: An Evangelical Theology of Renewal* (Downers Grove, IL: InterVarsity, 1979), 234, 252–53.

effecting individual conversion. Marsden believed that Dayton's depiction reoriented "these evangelicals' priorities [in] an unnecessary concession to the standards of twentieth-century liberal culture." In sum, Marsden contended, Dayton had made nineteenth-century revivalistic social reformers out to be more popular and more liberal than they actually were.[16]

Though it is true that those who stood up for the rights of women, African Americans, and other socially marginalized people were a minority of the religious population of the United States, nevertheless, this minority had an outsize impact on antebellum culture. Dayton never claimed that social activists were a majority of the nation, just that their views had more influence on modern revivalism—and ultimately on evangelicalism—than they have been given credit for.

Beyond the sphere of influence affected by Finney and his colleagues, the argument between Dayton and Marsden actually concerns something larger: the historiographical foundations of American evangelicalism as a whole. In essence, the debate hinges on whether US evangelicalism can best be interpreted through the lens of a Puritan/Old School Presbyterian/fundamentalist/neo-evangelical paradigm or a Pietist/New School Presbyterian/Methodist-Holiness/Pentecostal paradigm. Neither line of religious tradition, of course, should be construed as the only legitimate lens through which to observe evangelical history. Wesley and Edwards, Finney and Hodge, Phoebe Palmer and B. B. Warfield, William Seymour and Billy Sunday all influenced American evangelicalism. But a basic question continues to haunt the historiography: What is the primary way to understand evangelicalism—mental assent to certain inviolable doctrines and definitive views about the authority of the Bible or the living out of a particular kind of Christian piety that is informed by the gospel narrative and manifested in ethical activity? According to a study from 2005, neo-evangelical historians have claimed that "evangelicalism was synonymous with orthodoxy" and that the history of evangelicalism can best be discerned by studying Christians who perpetuated a

---

16. George Marsden, "Demythologizing Evangelicalism: A Review of Donald W. Dayton's *Discovering an Evangelical Heritage*," in *Christian Scholar's Review* 7 (1977): 203–7. Dayton's response: 207–10.

correct conservative theology, especially those rooted in Puritanism and its Reformed successors.[17] Dayton's argument is that the history of evangelicalism (at least in its eighteenth- and nineteenth-century embodiment) can be understood most clearly in light of an experiential core, in which born-again faith resulted in a distinct type of moral behavior. Dayton's accomplishment, then, was to "rediscover" a strand that had largely been obscured in the historical narratives, while Marsden objected that Dayton's elevation of the role of evangelical Pietist-activists overemphasized their historical significance.

A different critique is offered by D. G. Hart. Hart accepts Dayton's interpretation of evangelicalism as "something much bigger and broader" than the interpretation represented by neo-evangelical historians such as Marsden who "misrepresented evangelical history" with their "Reformed bias." If, however, evangelicalism is more diverse than often described by the "Reformed hegemony" in historiography, that doesn't mean that this expansive characterization of the movement is necessarily a good thing (in Hart's opinion) because the resulting, broadly defined evangelicalism is "more abstract and virtually meaningless." Hart thinks that Dayton's "gallery of evangelical reformers" is too diffuse since it includes people and events that were religiously "notorious" (Finney), theologically questionable (Weld, since he became a Unitarian at the end of his life), and historically "obscure" (such as the Lane Seminary revolt and the Oberlin civil disobedience case). Most bothersome to Hart is that Dayton seemed to agree with and promote Finney's "redemptive utopianism," even implying that the revivalist's quixotic ideas were "at the heart of the evangelical faith." By contrast, Hart contends that Finney "was deluded to think that such a[n idealistic] society could take root in America through revivalism's conversions and reforms." Finney's "staggering view of human potential and civil society" is incompatible with Hart's pessimism regarding the possibility of thoroughgoing personal or social transformation.[18]

17. See an analysis of neo-evangelical historiography in D. G. Hart, *Deconstructing Evangelicalism* (Grand Rapids: Baker Academic, 2005), 43–47, 50.

18. D. G. Hart, *From Billy Graham to Sarah Palin: Evangelicals and the Betrayal of American Conservatism* (Grand Rapids: Eerdmans, 2011), 84–91; Hart,

Finney's views regarding human nature did, in fact, move perilously close to a notion that individuals and society could perfect themselves. Most of his revivalist contemporaries, however, were more careful to insist that Christian perfection always starts with the work of God and then humans are invited to participate in that work. The majority of the social activists Dayton describes in the following chapters, then, were not Pelagians, who believed they could bring about the millennium unaided, but simply Arminians who were hopeful regarding God's intent to restore the earth through the agency of evangelical reform. Nonetheless, even that extent of confidence in the power of God's grace to renew this existing world, Hart believes, presents a profound theological problem. Hart, along with other theologically conservative Calvinists, is convinced not only that Finney was in error but also that all of Finney's social reform cohorts were.

If post-fundamentalist neo-evangelicals on the right have disagreed with Dayton's argument that the normative posture of nineteenth-century evangelicalism was a hopeful revivalistic piety issuing forth in social activism, so too have thinkers on the left who contend for greater social justice advocacy than what they perceive in nineteenth-century evangelicalism. These writers doubt that evangelicals (especially white evangelicals) were ever truly systemic in their social reform efforts. Rather than Finney and friends being too progressive, such critics maintain that they were not progressive enough. Michael Emerson and Christian Smith, for example, in an influential book titled *Divided by Faith*, assert that Finney was a compromiser on issues of race. And since Finney was an important evangelical forerunner, his policies affect today's evangelicalism, which continues to perpetuate racial division. Such scholars insist that white abolitionists (most of whom were evangelicals) were motivated by their guilt over complicity with slaveholding more than their concern for the human rights of African Americans. "Although calling for a people to be freed, they did not call for an end to racialization." Meanwhile, in regard to evangelical women, scholars such as Priscilla Pope-Levison have

"Jump In, the Post-Evangelical Water Is Warm (Even If the Pond Is Small)," *Old Life: Reformed Faith and Practice*, October 24, 2012, http://oldlife.org/2012/10/jump-in -the-post-evangelical-water-is-warm-even-if-the-pond-is-small/.

drawn attention to the mixed social reform legacy of some female Holiness evangelicals. The evangelist Alma White, for instance, acted in ways that were openly nativist and anti-Catholic at the same time that she pushed for women's rights.[19]

These scholars' points of view provide constructive nuance to Dayton's argument. Pope-Levison's analysis, for instance, helps us to recognize that Holiness women and men displayed a variety of attitudes and behaviors. And a closer look at Finney reveals that he sometimes prevaricated on issues of race. On occasion, he allowed congregational seating to be segregated. He also urged caution regarding the degree to which evangelical abolitionists engaged in politics, for fear that their political campaigning might eclipse their primary commitment to evangelistic preaching. While Finney insisted, on the one hand, that a revival could not occur unless churches took socially advanced views "in regard to any question involving human rights," he and many other evangelicals believed, on the other hand, that the conversion of individual men and women to personal faith took precedence over any other allegiance—including social transformation.[20]

Nonetheless, there are difficulties with these liberal criticisms of Finney and other nineteenth-century evangelical reformers. First, judging their motives and level of dedication by contemporary standards of social justice is anachronistic. It is true that the reformers were not always consistent; that their actions did not always reflect the high level of their rhetoric; that their urgent belief in the need for individuals to be evangelized sometimes trumped their commitment to social change; and that some of them espoused views that were not completely egalitarian. Nevertheless, their stances on race and gender inclusion were significantly advanced beyond what had been common in the previous generation, and their views were exceedingly more forward-thinking than the racist and sexist attitudes held by the

19. Michael O. Emerson and Christian Smith, *Divided by Faith: Evangelical Religion and the Problem of Race in America* (New York: Oxford University Press, 2000), 31–34; Beverly Eileen Mitchell, *Black Abolitionism: A Quest for Human Dignity* (Maryknoll, NY: Orbis, 2005), 128–30; Priscilla Pope-Levison, *Turn the Pulpit Loose: Two Centuries of American Women Evangelists* (New York: Macmillan, 2004), 138–39.

20. Charles G. Finney, *Lectures on Revivals of Religion* (New York: Fleming H. Revell, 1868), 272–73.

vast majority of their contemporaries. Perhaps the governing question should not be, How far from our standards of social inclusion were the evangelical abolitionists? but rather, How different were these people from the norm at the time? Indeed, Finney's opponents called him and his colleagues "radicals" and "ultraists" and regularly indicted them with the scandalous charge of inciting African Americans to think of themselves as equal to white Americans. As African American evangelical abolitionist Samuel Ringgold Ward wrote, referring to his white evangelical colleagues: "in the face of bad social customs, education, and religion, God enabled *some whites* to do and to endure all things for our cause."[21]

The debating and agitation of evangelical social activists popularized the connection of religious faith with social action and moved the mid-nineteenth-century ethical discussion along in ways that eventually led toward greater equality for women and people of color. Though structural understandings that later became common among twentieth-century social scientists were yet to be developed, evangelical social reformers nevertheless challenged systems of power, at least in a preliminary way, and provide an example that counters the claim that evangelicals inherently resist engagement with structural social change.[22]

A second difficulty with the criticism of some liberal scholars is their assertion that that nineteenth-century evangelicalism was a movement composed only, or at least primarily, of white men with conservative social attitudes. In contrast to this characterization, nineteenth-century evangelicalism was diverse: for starters, women made up the majority of the movement. Evangelical women became significant reform leaders—by their organizing, teaching, and even preaching. As Dayton recounts later in this book, small evangelical denominations such as the Wesleyan Methodists and the United Brethren affirmed

21. Samuel Ringgold Ward, *Autobiography of a Fugitive Negro* (1855; repr., Chicago: Johnson Publishing, 1970), 61. Emphasis in original.

22. Douglas M. Strong, *Perfectionist Politics: Abolitionism and the Religious Tensions of American Democracy* (Syracuse: Syracuse University Press, 1999), 131–36, 164–66; Ronald C. White Jr. and C. Howard Hopkins, *The Social Gospel: Religion and Reform in Changing America* (Philadelphia: Temple University Press, 1976), 3–25; Anthony L. Dunnavant, ed., *Poverty and Ecclesiology: Nineteenth-Century Evangelicals in the Light of Liberation Theology* (Collegeville, MN: Michael Glazier, 1993).

the public leadership of women decades before their counterparts in mainline denominations.

In terms of the racial composition of evangelicalism, the movement included large numbers of African Americans as well as whites. Most nineteenth-century African Americans considered themselves to be Christians in the revivalistic, evangelical sense described by Baird in *Religion in America*. They proclaimed and witnessed to a personal, biblically informed relationship with Jesus and preached the necessity of conversion to Christ. Indeed, many African American religious leaders—such as Amanda Berry Smith, Samuel Ringgold Ward (both mentioned later in this book), Zilpha Elaw, Julia Foote, Willis Hodges, Jermain Loguen, Daniel A. Payne, J. W. C. Pennington, Charles B. Ray, and Emma J. Ray—clearly identified themselves as evangelicals, in full partnership with their white brothers and sisters in the twin causes of Christian evangelism and social justice.[23]

And regarding white evangelicals, although it is true that many of them (in the North as well as the South) held to socially conservative positions, other white evangelicals became abolitionist agitators, a position always considered to be extremist by nineteenth-century standards. While some abolitionists, including Finney, stopped short of advocating complete racial amalgamation, other white evangelicals were thoroughly radical in their views of full racial equality and in their critique of white privilege. In the chapters that follow, Dayton describes such radical evangelicals as Catherine and William Booth, Luther Lee, B. T. Roberts, Orange Scott, Charles T. Torrey, and Theodore Weld. There were also others, not highlighted in this book, such as William Goodell, Beriah Green, Gilbert Haven, and Gerrit Smith. Similar to many evangelical abolitionists, Lewis Tappan forcefully spoke out against the sin of "prejudice" and "hateful caste feeling" that undergirded slavery, not only against the practice of slaveholding. For Tappan, there should be "honor in white and black the same," since all people bear the image of God. (By contrast, most nineteenth-century

23. Strong, *Perfectionist Politics*, 96, 101, 150, 163, 167; William L. Andrews, ed., *Sisters of the Spirit* (Bloomington: Indiana University Press, 1986), 2–16; Priscilla Pope-Levison, "Emma Ray in Black and White," *Pacific Northwest Quarterly* 102:3 (Summer 2011): 107–15.

"modernist" or theologically liberal opponents of revivalistic evangelicalism promoted an evolutionary view of racist Anglo-Saxon supremacy.) In yet another example that illustrates the social radicalism of evangelicals, a number of white Baptist and Methodist preachers in 1838 identified with their oppressed Cherokee co-religionists by vehemently opposing the forced relocation of Native Americans and, facing derision, accompanied the Natives on the infamous Trail of Tears. As a religious movement, then, nineteenth-century evangelicalism incorporated a range of people. While some evangelicals adapted to the prevailing culture, other evangelicals—including women and men, African Americans, Native Americans, and whites—spoke out and acted against the "principalities and powers" of that age.[24]

Dayton's Argument Popularized within the 1970s Context

When published in 1976, the first edition of *Discovering an Evangelical Heritage* created something of a sensation for younger adult Christians, arriving as it did at a pivotal juncture in American church history. During the previous decade of the 1960s, almost all who called themselves evangelicals (more accurately, post-fundamentalist neo-evangelicals) remained aloof—at best—from the protests regarding the Vietnam War, the fight for racial equality and civil rights, concerns about environmental degradation, and feminism. Some neo-evangelicals actively opposed these movements. But by the beginning of the 1970s, many twenty- and thirtysomething evangelicals felt they could no longer stay quiet regarding pressing justice issues.

Several factors propelled this 1970s shift in the evangelical subculture toward social activism, especially among disaffected college students and other young believers. The spiritual stirrings of the charismatic movement, for instance, propelled some experientially centered Christians to support justice concerns. Drawing from such diverse

24. Strong, *Perfectionist Politics*, 35, 132, 165; Laura Smith Haviland, *A Woman's Life-Work* (Cincinnati: Waldon and Stowe, 1882); Gary Dorrien, *The Making of American Liberal Theology: Imagining Progressive Religion, 1805–1900* (Louisville: Westminster John Knox, 2001), 314–29, 408–10; William G. McLoughlin, *Cherokees and Missionaries, 1789–1839* (New Haven: Yale University Press, 1984).

sources as Pentecostalism and the teachings of the Second Vatican Council, the charismatic renewal broke out in the 1960s in Protestant churches and on Catholic university campuses. Charismatics expected to receive a direct bolt of power from the Holy Spirit. They seemed disinterested in the propositional arguments of the neo-evangelicals; neither did they feel connected to the "cultural captivity" of conventional post–World War II mainline churches.[25] The ideology and teachings of liberal Protestantism did not appeal to charismatics. In their enthusiastic zeal, charismatics distrusted any rationalistic or culturally accommodating religion. The affective, therapeutic spirituality of the charismatics manifested many similarities to the emotive faith expression characteristic of pietistic nineteenth-century evangelicals.

The charismatic renewal opened the door to the Jesus movement, rooted in the California hippie culture's disenchantment with the status quo of American society. Though some exponents of the Jesus movement (Chuck Smith, for instance) eventually veered back to social conservatism or cultivated a personalistic gospel that demanded no social responsibility, the more typical attitude of the "Jesus freaks" reflected the institutional questioning inherent in the movement's antiestablishment origins. The desire for an ascetic, simple lifestyle, for example, led to intentional Christian communities, some of which became communal living experiments, such as the Shiloh youth revival centers, Reba Place Fellowship in Chicago, the Christian World Liberation Front in Berkeley, California, and hundreds of lesser-known communities. Even my rural hometown of just four thousand people had a charismatic, semi-intentional Christian community in the 1970s known as Celebration. (A communitarian precursor and model, though not charismatic, was the Church of the Saviour in Washington, DC, begun in the late 1940s by Gordon Cosby, which focused on inward contemplation and outward social-justice-oriented "mission groups" to the city.) Similarly, many students volunteered with Youth With A Mission, Operation Mobilization, World Vision, and other faith-based organizations such as the Mennonite Central Committee.

25. Clarence C. Goen, "The Cultural Captivity of the American Churches," *American Baptist Quarterly* (December 1991): 288–304.

Yet others—as epitomized by Ronald Sider's book *Rich Christians in an Age of Hunger*—denounced unbridled American consumerism.

The rise of Christian rock concerts represented a related development. As an alternative to Woodstock, new Christian believers established "Jesus Festivals" throughout the country. The first of these music events—the Ichthus festival, held in Wilmore, Kentucky, in 1970—began as the aftermath of a notable revival on the campus of Asbury College. The festival was the brainchild of Robert W. Lyon, a pacifist New Testament professor at neighboring Asbury Seminary. Donald Dayton was on the staff of Asbury Seminary in those years, during the same heady time that Gilbert James, another justice-minded professor at the seminary, influenced Dayton's vision of evangelical social witness. And Dayton preached about the heritage of piety and justice at the second Ichthus event in 1971.[26]

A parallel early Christian music festival, along with the formation of a rock group called Resurrection Band (Rez Band), grew out of the ministry of Jesus People USA. Founded in Chicago in 1972, Jesus People USA is one more example of countercultural evangelicalism developing from the original Jesus Movement. An observer described Jesus People USA as a "blend of Christian socialism, theological orthodoxy, postmodern theory, and an ethos of edgy artistic expression." The nonconformity of pioneering Christian rock musicians, such as Larry Norman and Randy Stonehill (who produced the first Christian rock albums), demonstrated that evangelicalism in the early 1970s had moved away from its relatively unified post-fundamentalist conservatism and had instead become a "diverse, complex movement."[27]

The civil rights movement also strongly affected evangelical social action. As mentioned, most African Americans were traditionally evangelical in their religious disposition—at least when the term is understood in the nineteenth-century pietistic sense Baird described.

26. Robert W. Lyon, "The L. O. Society at Asbury Theological Seminary," *Transformation* 3, no. 4 (October 1986): 10–14. Dayton dedicated *Discovering an Evangelical Heritage* to Gilbert James.
27. Shawn David Young, "From Hippies to Jesus Freaks: Christian Radicalism in Chicago's Inner-City," *Journal of Religion and Popular Culture* 22, no. 2 (Summer 2010): 1–28.

Since the vast majority of white neo-evangelicals avoided the civil rights struggle of the 1950s and '60s, however, African American evangelicals felt little affinity toward their fellow white believers. Nevertheless, some black Christian preachers in the late 1960s, such as Tom Skinner, William Pannell, William Bentley, and especially John Perkins, became known for both their evangelism and their civil rights activism. These leaders were joined by John Alexander, a young white evangelical whose publication *Freedom Now* drew the interest of a small number of whites and blacks.

A group of white Mississippi Methodist pastors who penned a protest statement against their state's virulent racism in 1963 provided a notable, but rare, example of prophetic evangelical courage. Tom Skinner and white evangelist Leighton Ford spoke out about racial division at the 1969 US Congress on Evangelism, and a similar focus by Skinner, Samuel Escobar, and David Howard enthralled the attendees at InterVarsity's Urbana conference in 1970. Eventually, in the early 1970s, a few more white evangelicals spoke out for civil rights, emboldened by the combination of faith and justice modeled by their African American brothers and sisters. Significantly, the struggle for racial equality prodded some late-twentieth-century Christians to look once again at the central role evangelicals played in the agitation against racism during the antebellum period. And neo-evangelicalism in the 1970s took tentative steps toward becoming more diverse when African Americans (such as Perkins, Skinner, and Pannell), Latinos (such as Escobar, Orlando Costas, and Rene Padilla), and women (such as Sharon Gallagher, Nancy Hardesty, and Roberta Hestenes) exhorted their fellow Christians to action.

Yet another decisive factor toward evangelical social justice in the 1970s involved the increase in political action by evangelicals. Partly because the last significant political push by Christian churches—the drive to prohibit the manufacture and use of alcohol—ended ignominiously in 1933, most mid-twentieth-century neo-evangelicals avoided overt politicizing. From the 1930s until the 1970s, conservative Christians stayed clear of partisan involvement, an ostensibly apolitical position that actually had the general effect of supporting the status quo. But a number of evangelical young adults, including students from leading neo-evangelical seminaries (Trinity, Fuller, Gordon-Conwell), became politically active in the early 1970s. This renewal of evangelical civic engagement began during the heated election campaign of 1972, when Ronald Sider established "Evangelicals for McGovern," a group that dared to connect pietistic faith with progressive politics. Richard Quebedeaux described activists such as Sider in his 1974 book, *The Young Evangelicals*. Richard Mouw wrote about political evangelism from a Reformed perspective; and at the National Prayer Breakfast in 1973, Mark Hatfield, an evangelical Republican senator from Oregon known for his support for civil rights, audaciously prayed for repentance of the "sin that scarred the national soul," referring to the Vietnam War. Other evangelicals entered politics, such as Congressman John Anderson and Paul B. Henry, Anderson's legislative aide and the son of neo-evangelical theologian Carl F. H. Henry.[28] A whole slew of subgroups—organizations such as Evangelicals for Social Action (established by Sider), magazines such as *The Other Side* (formerly *Freedom Now*), *Radix*, *Inside*, *Transformation*, *Daughters of Sarah*, and especially *Post American* magazine, edited by Wallis—encouraged advocacy for political and social change. (Dayton was the first book editor for *Post American*.)

In his introductory editorial for *Post American*, Wallis issued a pointed challenge to conventional US Christianity, a challenge that arose from "the questioning of a new generation . . . in the midst of a radical awakening." Wallis used the term "radical" eight times in this brief opening article. Such word choice indicated his conviction that Christian faith is grounded in a biblically based commitment to Jesus Christ and that such commitment "is a liberating force which has radical consequences for human life and society." Wallis contrasted "radical evangelicals" with "established evangelicals." Regarding the latter, Wallis wrote: "We fault a narrow orthodoxy that speaks of salvation but is often disobedient to the teaching of the prophets, who clearly state that faith divorced from a radical commitment to social justice is a mockery." But he did not leave mainline Christians

28. Paul B. Henry, *Politics for Evangelicals* (Valley Forge, PA: Judson Press, 1974), 80, 103–24.

off the hook. "We fault also a naïve and inadequate liberal theology which neglects man's need of personal transformation and liberation, perverts the historic content of the Christian faith and reduces Jesus Christ to a Galilean boy scout." Instead of these accommodations to "a materialistic faith which supports and sanctifies the values of American society rather than calling them into question," he spoke for his young evangelical colleagues when he affirmed that they wanted "to commit [them]selves to discipleship to Jesus Christ and the proclamation of the total Christian message of personal and social liberation . . . to be Christian and to be radical."[29]

Wallis found the story of nineteenth-century evangelical activists to be heartening. In the disappointing aftermath of Nixon's landslide reelection over McGovern, Wallis took encouragement in the "evidence that large numbers of Christians do believe that the gospel has necessary social and political consequences." In that light, Wallis provided his readers

> a little historical perspective. The evangelical movement of the last [nineteenth] century played a major role in the achievement of improved conditions for human life. Nineteenth century evangelism stimulated in the people a concern for social issues which resulted in the abolition of slavery, prison reform, humane treatment of the mentally ill, and improved working conditions for industrial laborers. There was at that time no dichotomy between spiritual renewal and social compassion.

He continued: "During the first few decades of this [twentieth] century a new [dispensational] theology was born which emphasized man's relation to God, and said very little about man's relation to man. No doubt this was partly due to the fact that much of liberal theology stressed social action and neglected personal transformation. But nothing can excuse the heresy that prides itself in preaching the true gospel, while refusing to apply that message to the totality of human affairs." Thankfully, Wallis reported, "the evangelical

29. Jim Wallis, "Post-American Christianity," in *Post American* 1, no. 1 (Fall 1971): 2–3; 3, no. 1 (January 1974): 1.

"Declaration of Evangelical Social Concern" (the "Chicago Declaration")

community was about to reverse the great reversal, and return to its historic, biblical stance."[30]

The pivotal event for this "new generation of radical Christians" was a gathering of (mostly) young leaders in November 1973 that

30. Wallis, *Post American* 1, no. 5 (Fall 1972): 1.

produced the Chicago Declaration of Evangelical Social Concern. Sider convened the group after gaining organizational experience with his efforts on behalf of Evangelicals for McGovern. The Chicago Declaration's fifty-three signatories included Dayton, Wallis, Sider, Perkins, Escobar, Gallagher, and others "whose faith is Christ centered," who "hold an unapologetic Biblical faith," and who share "a common spirit and commitment to the priorities of discipleship and the urgent need for an obedient and prophetic church." They saw themselves representing "new stirrings and directions in the evangelical church . . . the spreading of radical Christian consciousness."[31]

In the exhilarating period that followed the Chicago Declaration, Wallis asked Dayton to write ten articles for *Post American* in 1974–75 that would help young evangelicals position their activism within a larger historical context.[32] After the series ran in the magazine, Dayton assembled the articles into *Discovering an Evangelical Heritage*, published in 1976. Two other important evangelical books came out that same year on similar themes: Wallis's *Agenda for Biblical People*, a manifesto for social action among evangelicals, and Perkins's *Let Justice Roll Down*, about the need for a Jesus-centered movement for racial justice.

These three books, by Dayton, Wallis, and Perkins, appeared during the nation's bicentennial year, providing the immediate context for their reception—a fortuitous timing. As most of the United States prepared to celebrate the anniversary with unreserved patriotism by retelling the stories of traditional American heroes, other citizens, including young evangelicals, wanted to broadcast a fuller narrative regarding the nation's past. A different, more inclusive history began to be explored, as exemplified by the 1977 television series *Roots*, which sought to discover the background of formerly enslaved African American families.

In this setting, the evangelical songwriter Ken Medema composed an alternative musical number for the bicentennial that, according to

31. Wallis, *Post American* 3, no. 1 (January 1974): 1. See also David R. Swartz, *Moral Minority: The Evangelical Left in an Age of Conservatism* (Philadelphia: University of Pennsylvania Press, 2012).
32. *Post American* 3, no. 5 to iss. 4, no. 5 (June 1974–May 1975).

Medema, was intended "to bring another perspective on all the noise and grandstanding around the big 200th birthday bash."[33] Instead of writing an unvarnished paean to American illustriousness, Medema authored these more balanced lyrics in his song "I See America":

> I have seen the dauntless pilgrims who came from foreign
>   shores and braved the raging peril of the sea . . .
> But I've seen how first Americans were driven from their land
>   and I've seen the slave ships come from far away . . .
> I see America through the eyes of love; I long for all her
>   people to be free.
> And if you see, put your hand to the job for there is work that
>   must be done,
> Till freedom's song is sung and freedom's bell is rung from
>   sea to shining sea.[34]

Evangelicals like Medema still affirmed the possibility of hope in America, but they did so chastened by the events of the 1960s and were less sanguine about the positive intentions of the US government. Like the evangelical abolitionists who confronted the Fugitive Slave Law in the 1850s (see chapter 5), the 1970s social activists criticized their nation but also looked forward to the possibility of God's reign breaking forth.

In addition to the bicentennial celebration, 1976 was also a presidential election year, with a campaign dominated by an upstart, publicly evangelical candidate—Jimmy Carter. The Georgia governor appeared to embody a squeaky-clean break from the corruption-and-violence-stained decade that extended from the Birmingham church bombing and Kennedy's assassination through the agony of the Vietnam War and Watergate (1963–74). For many, Carter's earnest religious expression seemed to accentuate the promise of a new beginning for the country and for American Christianity. His opponent, Gerald Ford, also lifted up his evangelical credentials. (Ford's son studied at

33. Personal communication between Ken Medema and Douglas Strong, June 20, 2013.
34. Ken Medema, "I See America" on *Through the Eyes of Love*, Word Records, B00290W51G, 1977, vinyl.

Gordon-Conwell Theological Seminary.) Evangelicalism was recognized as an untapped, potent political force, especially since evangelical churches were adding members much faster in the 1970s than non-evangelical churches. *Newsweek* dubbed 1976 "The Year of the Evangelicals," particularly because of the way in which Carter's Southern Baptist piety and social progressivism represented an unexpected twist on the usual pejorative perception of evangelicalism. Educated Americans could no longer view evangelicalism as a backcountry artifact gradually giving way to the cultural dominance of mainline Protestantism. The unabashed faith of both presidential candidates symbolized evangelicalism's 1970s rise out of obscurity. But this public rehabilitation could only have happened because of the emergence of a different kind of evangelical—an enthusiastic, activist, even radical evangelical spirit. Many of these new evangelicals took their inspiration from their nineteenth-century forebears, and *Discovering an Evangelical Heritage* gave them the material to use. Arriving during the bicentennial and the election of a self-professed evangelical president, this book was a tract for the times.

Immediately after this introduction, you will find the preface Donald Dayton wrote for the 1988 reprint of the first edition. His original (1976) prologue and chapters follow in succession. In these chapters the reader will quickly perceive the effect that Dayton's message had among socially active Christians in the 1970s and '80s—and also how that message may become similarly transformative among faithful people today.

Preface to the Reprint
of the First Edition (1988)

By Donald W. Dayton

I write this preface for a reprint of the first edition of *Discovering an Evangelical Heritage* shortly after attending my twenty-fifth college reunion (*not* at Wheaton College—as so many of the reviewers of the original publication assumed because of the first chapter) and in the midst of something of a revival of interest in the issues and culture (music, persons, etc.) of the 1960s. Both experiences have impressed on me the wisdom of those who have insisted that this book be reprinted, not only because of the wide use that it has found in classrooms, but also because of the continuing relevance of the issues with which it deals.

In the dozen years since its original publication I have been astonished at the reception that has been accorded this small book, which was originally prepared as a series of essays for *Sojourners* magazine (then the *Post American*) by a young graduate student who I now think made his professors a little nervous by making his publishing debut in such a format, without the usual scholarly apparatus. To my surprise the book made *Eternity* magazine's list of the twenty-five most important books of the year. And since then I have been gratified by the response to the book—in the diversity of places it has been used (ranging from Bible colleges through liberal seminaries to a Marxist commune) and in the range of classes (from Sunday schools through graduate school) in which it has found a role (from "evangelical studies" through "women's studies" to "social ethics"). I was especially moved by some of the responses to the book in travels abroad (from Latin America through Europe to South Africa), where I was told that a book that I had thought to be peculiarly North American was full of relevance to other contexts. But most of all I have treasured the many people who have written to express their appreciation for the personal tone of the book in revealing my own pilgrimage and struggle in ways that enabled the book to touch their own experience and to help resolve questions of identity and evangelical commitment.

All of this has made the task of revision especially difficult—and indeed conflicts over the extent and character of revisions with the original publisher are a large part of the reason for the delay of this reprint and its appearance with another publisher. I am pleased that Hendrickson Publishers (in particular David Townsley, with whom I first discussed the idea, editor Patrick Alexander, with whom I have worked, and founder and president Stephen Hendrickson) has agreed that the book needed to be available again. Hendrickson is a publisher with roots in the Pentecostal tradition that is a major carrier of the concerns and to some extent the theology of the theological traditions celebrated in this book. This reprint is thus a happy marriage of content and publisher.

Some reviewers noticed a certain energy and advocacy in the book. For some this was a lamentable lapse into "soap-box" history; for others it was a refreshing "enlivening" of history that made the book more useful for the average person outside the academic world. For the former I would be glad to share the letters from historians of the movements involved testifying to its accuracy and objectivity—or the review by one astonished reader who attempted independent verification and concluded that I had if anything understated my case. I have become more and more convinced that most historical writing is implicitly a form of advocacy or a search for a "usable history." I have tried to be more self-conscious about this fact than many historians of the "evangelical experience"—and thus have been reluctant to change or omit the prologue, which from the beginning I have considered an essential part of this book.

This book has been reprinted [in 1988] essentially without change and needs to be understood in terms of its place in my own pilgrimage and against the backdrop of the cultural struggles alluded to in the prologue. Personal experience and cultural questions can open up true insights into Christian experience and the Scriptures as well as obscure them. The question is not whether the book is rooted in a specific experience (it obviously is—as are all writings whether such is acknowledged or not), but whether there is value in the insights into Christian truth and experience that are to be found therein. But this fact has made revision difficult in that little changes threatened to unravel the whole and require a new book. It seemed preferable to keep the book as it is and to let it be read in terms of the histories (personal and cultural) out of which it arose.

This decision was confirmed by the fact that in several rereadings I found very little to revise. The few times that I use the word "recent" to refer to events that are now a little less recent should not be too distracting. The only substantive change that I might make now would be to indicate in chapters 2 and 8 that many of the "new measures" of the revivalism of evangelist Charles Grandison Finney were probably borrowings from earlier Methodism that became more visible and controversial when adopted by Presbyterians. (I now see that it's an interesting comment on evangelical historiography and on those who do the writing that such things as the ministry of women apparently really only begin to happen when they happen in the circles of those cultural elites who write most about such things!) Other than this I would not wish to change a single line in the book. I stand behind what I have said in both detail and general interpretation.

I would like to call attention to the title. I continue to be amazed at the ways in which it is repeatedly cited incorrectly. My own original working title was *Whatever Happened to Good Old-Fashioned Evangelicalism?*, but that was not acceptable to the original publisher. I proposed *Rediscovering an Evangelical Heritage*, but had to give up the "re-" as an apparent redundancy that offended the publisher's sensitivities. The irony has been the number of times it has been cited as "Rediscovering." [The 2014 second edition has restored the word "Rediscovering" to the title.] No matter; I see the point. More significant is the "an" (rather than "the" or "our" that is often substituted in citations) that I had to fight for to make clear my own understanding of the limited claims of the book. I understand very well that there are other strands of what might be called "evangelicalism." But I do insist that I am working directly with the fountainhead of modern revivalism and thus with the central tradition of what most people mean by "evangelicalism." Probably the greatest change in the book or its title if it were to be rewritten today would be an increasing doubt about the use of the word "evangelical" and its ability to communicate today. I am even more impressed today by the contrast and even contradiction between the way in which the word was used in the nineteenth century (and is still carried perhaps most consistently in my own Wesleyan tradition) and the way in which the word is used today by the "neo-evangelicals" in the wake of fundamentalism. This issue is discussed in the epilogue; and here I only indicate the continuing relevance of this point for the understanding of the book.

Those who wish to understand the issues better may wish to follow the discussion in what I consider to be the most useful review/dialogue with the book by George Marsden (who has since emerged as a major interpreter of the evangelical/fundamentalist experience) under the title "Demythologizing Evangelicalism" in *Christian Scholar's Review*, volume 7 (1977): 203–10. There Marsden follows the "neo-evangelical" line to suggest that "evangelical" should be understood as the "orthodox" or "traditional" wing of Protestantism that resisted "modernity" and the rise of "liberalism." This position is difficult to reconcile with, among other things, the data I bring forth in chapter 8 about the widespread ministry of women in "evangelical" circles (continued especially in Holiness and Pentecostal churches)—a nontraditional practice that sets such "evangelical" groups apart from the "traditional" Protestant churches that are only now beginning to move toward such practices. In my view (developed somewhat in the above-mentioned *CSR* dialogue) "evangelicalism" is better understood as a specific wing of the nineteenth-century revivalist tradition that took shape before the emergence of fundamentalism and along different lines—and that the fundamentalist experience will be understood finally only when it takes such issues into account. This difference between my perspective and those working more directly out of the "neo-evangelical" tradition has become increasingly important to me. In part the issue is in the sources that we use to develop our interpretations. Marsden tends to work with the more elite Presbyterian and Baptist traditions, while I find the more grassroots Methodist (and ensuing Holiness and Pentecostal) traditions more illuminating for the interpretation of the "evangelical experience." Those who are interested in how my thinking has continued on these questions are referred to *Theological Roots of Pentecostalism* (Scarecrow Press and Francis Asbury Press of Zondervan, 1987), which I intended as something of an "alternative historiography of evangelicalism" as well as a study of the topic announced in the title. I have attempted to spell out some of the historiographical issues in an essay titled "Yet Another Layer of the Onion: Or Opening the Ecumenical Door to Let the Riffraff In" (*Ecumenical Review*, January 1988). I suspect that the issues will be even more discussed in the future. (They were pursued in a systematic way in the 1990s under the sponsorship of the Wesleyan/Holiness Study Project at Asbury Theological Seminary with funding from the Pew Foundation.) I find that the questions and issues that have driven me toward this "historical revisionism" are found in kernel here in *Discovering an Evangelical Heritage*.

Probably the single most important development since the book first appeared has been the heightened public awareness of the influence of the "New Religious Right" and the associated "electronic church" with its own form of social and political activism. I am often asked how such relates to this book—sometimes with the tongue-in-cheek suggestion that I have been too successful in calling "evangelicals" to political and social engagement; I doubt there is much connection between this book and the Religious Right, but full treatment of the question is beyond the limits of this preface. There certainly are continuities—particularly along the lines of issues of morality and vice—between the earlier period and the contemporary phenomenon. But there are also significant differences that seem important to me—especially the tendency of the movements of the 1980s to major on issues of personal morality and vice and to neglect the issues of poverty and justice that were more to the fore in the nineteenth century. In a sense the 1980s movements sometimes seem to be more committed to an ethic of the "preservation" of supposed "Christian values" in an age in which these are being eroded than to the extension of justice and the concern to follow the biblical mandate to identify with the "poor and oppressed." (For me chapter 9 is perhaps the most important in this book.) But the issue is very complicated, and though I do not entirely sympathize with the new Religious Right, I do think that we have something to learn from it—and that it needs more sympathetic treatment than it tends to get from the secular media and from some other Christians.

I have also struggled with how much to revise the bibliography. There is a sense in which the original bibliography was a substitute for footnotes rather than a guide to the literature on the theme. As a guide to the literature, it is now, of course, somewhat dated. There is a new history of Wheaton College (chapter 1), finally a substantive biography of Finney (chapter 2), a new biography of Theodore Weld (chapter 3), a plethora of new literature on the women mentioned in chapter 8 (for an expansion of the argument in this chapter see Nancy Hardesty, *Women Called to Witness: Evangelical Feminism in the 19th Century*, Abingdon, 1984), and so forth. I have decided to leave the bibliography as it was—in the nature of footnotes so that those who want to trace my steps can follow in terms of the actual literature on which the book is based. Some of the literature behind this book has been reissued in facsimile reprints under my editorship in a series titled "The Higher Christian Life" (Garland Publishing). I have also been coediting with Kenneth Rowe of Drew University a monograph series "Studies in Evangelicalism" (Scarecrow Press). Several of the books in that series expand on themes in this book.

Perhaps I should mention, in view of what I make in chapter 2 of the expurgated editions of Finney's works, that Bethany Fellowship asked me after the publication of this book to edit an unexpurgated edition of Finney's "Letters of Revival." This is available as Charles G. Finney, *Reflections on Revival* (Bethany Fellowship, 1979) and contains the missing letter that I quote in chapter 2 as well as other material. And finally, I would like to dedicate this reprint to my son, Charles Soren Dayton, whose name expresses something of my own complicated spiritual pilgrimage and my own admiration for Charles Finney.

August 1988
Donald W. Dayton
Professor of Theology and Ethics
Northern Baptist Theological Seminary
Lombard, Illinois

Prologue to the First Edition (1976)

On Coming to Maturity in an Evangelical College in the 1960s

BY DONALD W. DAYTON

Whether the fact is admitted or not, most books arise out of the author's personal history. This book is no exception. In an age perhaps excessively conscious of the subliminal influence of social and psychic history on one's thinking and sensitivities, fairness to the reader requires frankness about the life situation behind one's writing. This book is a product of the author's struggle to reconcile the seemingly irreconcilable in his own experience: the evangelical heritage in which he was reared and values bequeathed him by the student movements of the 1960s.

The cultural trauma of the 1960s is now the common heritage of all America—and much of the world! That decade saw wave after wave of social protest and the emergence of new movements for justice and equality: the civil rights movement with its sit-ins, freedom rides, marches, confrontations, and deaths; the great revulsion against the

Vietnam War expressed in protest, draft resistance, draft-card burn-
ings, exiled youth, and conspiracy trials; and the discovery of unno-
ticed minorities and a history of neglect and oppression that tarnished
the images of the United States on which we had been nourished in
grade school. Few would defend all that happened in the 1960s, but
most would allow that in that decade fundamental principles came
to light that can no longer be ignored. There was no going back to
the innocence of the 1950s.

There was, however, in the 1960s at least one relatively safe bastion
of escape from this turmoil—the subculture that despite its diversity
is encompassed by the label "evangelical." The basic transmitters of
this tradition are a series of "Christian colleges" (some independent
and some denominationally anchored). These schools, usually situated in rural, small-town, or suburban locations, are scattered across
the country but tend to cluster in the Midwest. They are not widely
known, but their names (Wheaton, Houghton, Malone, Greenville,
Seattle Pacific, etc.) are revered within evangelicalism as fortresses
against the modern world, in which evangelical youth can be educated
and mate without threat from the pagan ideologies and lifestyles of
the secular world.

It is difficult to re-create the atmosphere of such a college in the
1960s. No doubt the incidents that loom so large in memory were
not the whole of campus life. But the contrast between the petti-
ness of the issues that troubled us and the magnitude of the issues
that were being dealt with in society is frightening. Campus life was
circumscribed by cultural patterns and ethical mores called "pru-
dentials" at my college. These included the traditional evangelical
prohibitions against drinking, smoking, dancing, card-playing, and
theater-going. Our lives were largely bound up in testing the limits of
these prohibitions. While other students responded to calls for civil
rights workers or took to the streets in protest about Vietnam, we
fought our administration over whether the yearbook could picture
male swimmers without T-shirts, struggled for the right to watch
TV in the lounge on Sundays, and wondered if the Christian should
attend the theater (legitimate or cinema) or read twentieth-century
literature.

We tended to be apolitical, but when political instincts did surface, they were conservative. Like most evangelicals of the decade, we supported Richard Nixon and Barry Goldwater in presidential elections. I was aware of only one voice of dissent on campus, a rather moderate Democrat who was harassed into leaving over his "liberal" political views and questionings of the campus ethos. Our great fear was Communism, and we found signs of its influence everywhere. We believed that the protest movements were manipulated by Communist agitators. Our editorial complaints that the campus lacked sufficient diversity for the dialogue that was an essential part of any liberal education were interpreted as the first steps in a campaign to bring a Communist speaker to campus or even to start a Communist cell.

Cultural insularity and reactionary social perspectives converged to produce what John Oliver of Malone College termed "A Failure of Evangelical Conscience."[1] Evangelical Christianity rather consistently opposed currents of the 1960s that demanded social justice and civil rights. Oliver traced this through the editorial pages of *Christianity Today*, the journal that spoke for evangelicalism in that decade. Claiming to represent the "biblical point of view," the editors defended "voluntary segregation," charged of Martin Luther King that "communism . . . is implicit in his integrationist ideology," condemned categorically demonstrations and civil disobedience, decried as a "mob spectacle" the 1963 March on Washington at which Martin Luther King delivered his famous "I Have a Dream" speech, praised Mississippi's refusal to admit black student James Meredith to its state university, and were horrified at the suggestion of interracial marriage. Concerning the war in Vietnam, the editors supported the American presence, stating that it was necessary for the security of Christian missions. They rebuked the critics of the war and called for the enforcement of laws against destroyers of draft cards and records while insisting that justice be "tempered with mercy" for those convicted of war crimes. They denied that the United States had any economic or

1. John Oliver, "A Failure of Evangelical Conscience," *Post American*, May 1975: 26–30. To keep scholarly apparatus to a minimum, only material from modern, secondary literature has been documented. The bibliography indicates the major sources consulted in the preparation of each chapter.

other "ulterior motives" for its presence in Indochina. The journal, of course, altered its position on most of these issues, but only in response to a reversal of popular consensus or official national policy.

The full significance of this "failure of evangelical conscience" has yet to be understood. To many of us, the civil rights movement and its principles of fundamental human equality seemed not only more right but also more biblical and Christian than the positions taken by our elders. We learned that what had been claimed as biblical and therefore absolute was often the deification of cultural patterns not only relative but in some cases even pernicious and demonic. Sizable contingents of several generations of evangelical college students responded to these insights by leaving the orbit of evangelicalism. Those that did not abandon the Christian faith altogether have found places of service in other parts of the church.

The trauma generated by these conflicts was intense. Torn between evangelicalism and the imperatives of the civil rights movement, I chose the latter—though troubled with a continuing "bad conscience" acquired through years of conditioning in the evangelical world. I worked with the Mississippi Freedom Democratic party in the election of 1964, I lived with blacks on the edge of Harlem during the riots of the summer of 1964, and I identified in successive years with various black churches and inner-city ministries. Cut loose from evangelicalism, I threw myself into the secular education of Columbia University and went to Yale Divinity School, seeking a theological reconstruction that could bring my intellectual world back together. In several years of study and experience I found that reformulation in the recovery of a biblically grounded and classically Christian faith amenable to the development of social responsibility—and even a biblically grounded "Christian radicalism."

Having established an independent standpoint, I was able to look back on evangelicalism with some equanimity. In what was intended to be a casual aside in a graduate program in theology, I took up the study of the roots of the denomination in which I had been reared. Though never helped to understand its history in college or in church life, I discovered much to my surprise that the denomination was a product of the closest parallel to the civil rights movement in American history—the abolitionist protest against slavery in the pre–Civil War period. The founders of my denomination and college were advocates of principles in which I had come to believe by a very indirect route. As I pursued this story, I discovered the sweet irony that this denomination was not unique, but shared a reformist heritage with other aspects of evangelicalism. I had been struggling with the wrong end of evangelical currents that had once reverberated with vitality and reform activity, but had over the course of a century fallen into a form of decadence. This book is an overview of that history—a history that has forced me to rethink, not only my own relationship to evangelicalism, but also the broader significance of that movement in American culture.

1

Jonathan Blanchard

The Radical Founder of Wheaton College

If there is a single symbol of modern evangelicalism, it is Wheaton College, situated just to the west of Chicago in the "All-American City" of Wheaton, Illinois. This school of about two thousand students is the most prestigious and perhaps the oldest of the "Christian colleges" that lie at the core of evangelical culture and tradition. The city of Wheaton is itself a mecca for evangelicals. Headquartered here and in the surrounding area are many of the publishers, independent mission boards, and interdenominational agencies that compose the network of evangelical life and activity. Also in Wheaton are the offices of the National Association of Evangelicals, an "ecumenical" organization founded in 1942 that, by the 1970s, drew together some thirty denominations in an evangelical counterpart to the National Council of Churches.

Closely associated with the post–World War II neo-evangelical renaissance of scholarship that spawned the National Association of Evangelicals, Fuller Theological Seminary in Pasadena, and

Christianity Today, Wheaton College was the alma mater of many leaders of mid-twentieth-century neo-evangelicalism. Among these were Harold Lindsell, editor of *Christianity Today*; Edward J. Carnell, Fuller apologist and philosopher of religion; and Carl F. H. Henry, founding editor of *Christianity Today*. But the most famous alumnus of Wheaton College is evangelist Billy Graham, class of 1943. Through his position on the board of trustees and in other ways Graham was a dominant force in the life of the college—as in all of the evangelical world.

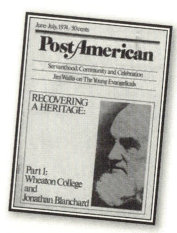

Billy Graham rather consistently expressed what may be taken to be the position of the National Association of Evangelicals, *Christianity Today*, much of Wheaton College, and most of the evangelical world: that the primary mission of the church is the spiritual one of preaching a gospel of "personal salvation"

1974 Post American *cover (highlighting Donald Dayton's first serialized article, on Jonathan Blanchard)*

through faith in the atonement of Christ. Social witness may be an extension of the life of the individual, regenerated person in society but should not be incorporated into the life of the church as a primary goal.

Graham expressed this position in a "clarification" issued early in 1973. When the peace negotiations in Paris broke down and the United States resumed its bombing of North Vietnam, a number of American churchmen appealed openly to the evangelist to use his friendship with President Richard Nixon to try to stop the bombing. In his response Graham said:

> I am convinced that God has called me to be a New Testament evangelist, not an Old Testament prophet! While some may interpret an evangelist to be primarily a social reformer or political activist, I do

not! An evangelist is a proclaimer of the message of God's love and grace in Jesus Christ and of the necessity of repentance and faith. My primary goal is to proclaim the Good News of the Gospel of Jesus Christ. The basic problem of man is within his own heart. That is why evangelism is so important.[1]

This position is generally assumed to be what evangelicals have always believed. To some extent this is true. But while Billy Graham sometimes uses the language of repentance and faith to avoid questions of social responsibility, earlier generations of evangelicals understood that repentance involved turning from apathy into the heart of struggles for social reform. While Billy Graham contrasts the "New Testament evangelist" and the "Old Testament prophet," earlier evangelicals combined these roles. One of the most significant figures of that earlier generation was Jonathan Blanchard, the founder of Wheaton College.

The central building on the Wheaton College campus is Blanchard Hall. At the top of a split winding staircase just inside the main entrance are two plaques honoring the men for whom the building is named. These men are Jonathan Blanchard and Charles A. Blanchard, father and son, the first and second presidents of Wheaton. These two men held the office for more than twenty and forty years, respectively. Together they guided Wheaton College through its first sixty-five years.

Each plaque contains a quotation that calls into question the evangelical perspective expressed by Billy Graham. On the plaque honoring Charles Blanchard is an affirmation of the reformist aspiration of youth.

> The need of a developing nation is to increase in wisdom, righteousness and strength and to cast off whatever is inconsistent with that noble age to which youth aspires. Only that which is true and right can abide. (From an address on the Day of Prayer for Colleges, "The American College")

More striking is the quotation on the plaque honoring Jonathan Blanchard, the founder of Wheaton College. It is taken from an address titled "A Perfect State of Society," originally delivered before the

---

1. Billy Graham, "A Clarification," *Christianity Today*, January 19, 1973, 36.

Society of Enquiry during the commencement exercises of Oberlin
College in 1839. (The significance of Oberlin will emerge later, in
chaps. 4 and 5). The plaque reads:

> Society is Perfect where what is right in theory exists in fact; where
> Practice coincides with Principle, and the Law of God is the Law of
> the Land.

This passage is the thesis of Blanchard's address in which he treated
"not so much the principles of the doctrines of Christ, as the form
they will give society, when they have done their perfect work upon
mankind." Among the affirmations of Blanchard at Oberlin was that
"every true minister of Christ is a universal reformer, whose business
it is, so far as possible, to reform all the evils which press on human
concerns." Blanchard fully realized that one "cannot construct a perfect society out of imperfect men," but argued that "every reformer
needs a perfect state of society ever in his eye, as a pattern to work
by, so far as the nature of his materials will admit."

This somewhat utopian vision was grounded in a doctrine of the
kingdom of Christ reflected in the Wheaton College motto, "For
Christ and his Kingdom." Blanchard understood the kingdom of God
as "Christ ruling in and over rational creatures who are obeying him
freely and from choice, under no constraint but that of love" and
argued that what "John the Baptist and the Saviour meant when they
preached the 'kingdom of God'" was "a perfect state of society." He
opposed those who emphasized that such a kingdom is not to be
sought in this world, insisting that though "this kingdom is not *of* this
world, it is *in* it." Carrying this affirmation to its logical conclusion,
Blanchard warned against both those who "locate Christ's kingdom
in the future to the neglect of the present" and those who seek "to
construct a local heaven upon earth, . . . thus shutting out the influences and motives of eternity."

Prompted by this vision of a "perfect state of society" and compelled by obedience to Christ's command to "seek ye first the kingdom
of God," Blanchard was propelled into a life of reform that climaxed
in the founding of Wheaton College. His life was so dominated by

reform that upon his death the *Political Dissenter* commented that "in the death of Dr. Jonathan Blanchard, American reformers have lost one of their foremost leaders. No more fearless voice ever rang out on the platform, or from the pulpit. No keener or more valiant pen has been wielded against popular wrongs, and in defense of unpopular truth."

Born in Vermont in 1811 and a graduate of Middlebury College, Blanchard studied theology at Andover Theological Seminary. There he came under the influence of Theodore Weld (for the significance of Weld, see chap. 3) and became, in the words of the *Dictionary of American Biography*, a "violent abolitionist." When the administration of Andover tried to stop his antislavery work, Blanchard withdrew and spent a year in Pennsylvania working as an agent for the American Anti-Slavery Society. (Agents were "agitators" who traveled around lecturing and organizing local chapters of abolitionists.) Blanchard endured mob violence, threats on his life, and other forms of abuse in this work. He then finished his education at Lane Theological Seminary in Cincinnati, where he continued his abolitionist activities. Upon graduation he was called to pastor Cincinnati's Sixth Presbyterian Church, a congregation widely known as the "nigger church" for its abolitionism. In spite of Blanchard's reformist orientation, the church added during his seven-year pastorate some five hundred members to the original one hundred twenty.

Blanchard's commitment to reform soon propelled him into an important leadership role among the abolitionists. He held office in the Ohio Anti-Slavery Society. In 1843 he was elected to the American vice presidency of the World's Anti-Slavery Convention in London. In 1845 he was called upon to represent the Cincinnati Abolition Society by debating against N. L. Rice the affirmative of the proposition that "slaveholding is in itself sinful and the relationship between master and slave a sinful relationship." This debate, in Cincinnati's largest auditorium and lasting several days, was widely advertised and published in a five-hundred-page book that went through several editions. This work is so important for understanding the abolitionist movement that several twentieth-century publishers reprinted it as a major resource for black studies programs.

After this debate Blanchard carried his reform ideas and work into education. For twelve years he served as president of Knox College in Galesburg, Illinois. After controversy forced his resignation, he was offered the presidency of a half dozen other colleges, but he eventually accepted the position at Wheaton. This school had actually been started in 1848 as Illinois Institute by the Wesleyan Methodists, an abolitionist body that had split from Methodism in 1843 over the question of slavery. (See chap. 7 for a discussion of the Wesleyan Methodists.) A few years later the Congregationalists joined the Wesleyans in support of the young institution, and when the Wesleyans failed to muster sufficient financial support, the college was rechartered in 1860 under Congregational control.

This change was made only after a covenant that Wheaton would continue Wesleyan reform principles. These were expressed in an advertisement for the college that appeared in 1859, vowing to preserve "the testimony of God's word against slave-holding, secret societies and their spurious worships, against intemperance, human inventions in church government, war, and whatever else shall clearly appear to contravene the kingdom and coming of our Lord Jesus Christ." Jonathan Blanchard was one person whom all could agree upon to be president of the college. His reformist temperament promised the continuation of the ideals upon which Wheaton was to be established. Blanchard accepted the invitation, and, as he put it himself, "I came to Wheaton in 1860, still seeking 'a perfect state of society' and a college 'for Christ and his Kingdom.'" And to Wheaton he gave the rest of his life.

Blanchard grounded his vision for the Christian college in the prophetic texts of Scripture. He pointed to the "schools of the prophets" where the "ancient people of Jehovah sent up their youth to learn the pure principles and practical application of his law." In those schools, according to Blanchard, the "truth of God" was explained to young "prophets" who were to see that this truth was "faithfully applied to correct the follies and the errors of the nation."

Blanchard's position on reform can best be understood through an examination of the Cincinnati debate. He affirmed the radical equality of the slaves in these words: "I rest my opposition to slavery upon the one-bloodism of the New Testament. All men are equal, because they are of one equal blood." He argued that slavery was a sin to be immediately abolished and suggested that church discipline be brought to bear upon those who held slaves or supported the institution of slavery. He did not view the question of slavery as an individual matter of personal purity, but insisted that "slave-holding is not a solitary, but a social sin," deserving attack on all fronts.

But we must also understand the position of his opponent, N. L. Rice. Though Blanchard attempted to brand him an advocate of slavery, Rice insisted that he, too, was an abolitionist, but committed to gradual abolition and "colonization" (sending the slaves back to Africa). He feared that the radical abolitionists were pushing too hard and were "upturning the very foundations of society in order to abolish slavery." He expressed concern for the "spiritual welfare" of slaves and slaveholders. He argued that if Southern ministers should become abolitionist, they would be expelled and all would be left without the "preaching of the gospel." Rice was concerned that the minister not move too far ahead of his congregation.

Blanchard insisted that Rice's position made his "religion . . . the religion of a privileged class" by perpetuating an evil system. Blanchard maintained that the churches and individual Christians must radically identify with the oppressed and wished after his death to be remembered only as "one who having humbly striven in all things to follow his Lord, like Him, also has been faithful to His poor" (Blanchard's final words in the Cincinnati debate).

Controversy still rages over whether the abolitionists were misguided fanatics or clear-sighted moral reformers. Earlier historiography dismissed them and bewailed their tendency to bring into the arena of public policy moral absolutes that could not be accommodated to the compromises of political solutions. Sensitized by the 1960s, scholars in the 1970s took a more sympathetic look at the abolitionists and discovered one of the most profound reform movements in American history—a movement that was largely grounded in evangelical Christianity.

But whatever modern American historians may decide about the abolitionists, it is clear that Blanchard was completely on their side.

He called the abolitionists "honest, simple-hearted, and clear-sighted; but few of them dwellers in high places; who take up the truth and the cross with it, to bear both after Christ." Indeed, he went so far as to identify the early Christians as "a poor despised set of abolitionists who were everywhere accused of 'uprooting society' to get rid of its evils, and *turning the whole world upside down*' to correct its errors and reform its abuses."

The debate between Blanchard and Rice was not between an abolitionist and a proslavery defender of the status quo, but between two divergent strategies for the elimination of slavery. Rice viewed Blanchard as an extremist upsetting the gradual process of amelioration of slavery effected by the preaching of the gospel, while Blanchard viewed Rice as a compromising equivocator unwilling to act on the radical implications of the gospel. To use more modern terminology, it would appear that Jonathan Blanchard, the founding president of Wheaton College, was, at least on the issue of slavery, a radical rather than a liberal.

2

Reform in the Life
and Thought of Evangelist
Charles G. Finney

Jonathan Blanchard, however, was not a lone voice for reform in his age. He was part of a much larger movement that combined the roles of "New Testament evangelist" and "Old Testament prophet." Wheaton College was only one manifestation of a revival movement that reached back to the pre–Civil War evangelism of Charles G. Finney, the father of modern revivalism. The Blanchards were among his disciples, and Wheaton College understood itself to stand in his succession. As late as the 1940s and '50s, V. Raymond Edman, Wheaton's fourth president, called the evangelical world back to Finney as "the most widely known and most successful American revivalist."[1] Edman's book *Finney Lives On* carried an endorsement by Billy Graham.

1. V. Raymond Edman, *Finney Lives On: The Secret of Revival in Our Time* (Wheaton: Scripture Press, 1951), 15.

Charles Grandison Finney, however, was greater than either the secular caricature of a ranting, hellfire evangelist or the evangelical images of a deeply spiritual preacher given totally to the "saving of souls."

Charles Grandison Finney: President of Oberlin College, revivalist, social reformer

In the words of American historian Richard Hofstadter of Columbia University, he "must be reckoned among our great men."[2] Though first and foremost an evangelist, Finney's work and the way he understood the gospel "released a mighty impulse toward social reform"[3] that shook the nation and helped destroy slavery.

Born in 1792 in Connecticut, Finney was reared in central New York in what has come to be known as the "burned over district"—so called because "revival fires" so often swept the area. After two years of education in a Connecticut academy, he returned to upstate New York to study, and eventually to practice, law. Well on his way to a successful legal career, Finney began to study the Bible to better understand law-book references to Mosaic legislation. The result of this reading (and the prayers and entreaties of his fiancée) was a spiritual struggle climaxing in a profound conversion. The morning after his initial religious experience, Finney announced a new vocation to a startled client: "Deacon, I have a retainer from the Lord Jesus Christ to plead his cause and I cannot plead yours."

At the age of twenty-nine Finney began informal study for the ministry. Within a few years he was ordained and was gaining a national

2. Richard Hofstadter, *Anti-Intellectualism in American Life* (New York: Alfred A. Knopf, 1964), 92.

3. Gilbert Hobbs Barnes, *The Anti-Slavery Impulse 1830–1844*, repr. ed. with new introduction by William G. McLoughlin (New York: Harcourt, Brace and World, 1964), 11.

reputation as an evangelist through his work in upstate New York. By the early 1830s Finney was preaching to large crowds in Philadelphia, Boston, and New York. In 1835 he published his *Lectures on Revivals of Religion*, reissued in a 1960 critical edition by Harvard University Press as a determinative force in the shaping of American culture. Also in 1835, Finney was invited to become professor of theology at the newly founded Oberlin College. Except for frequent revival trips to New York, England, and elsewhere, Finney spent the rest of his life in Oberlin, becoming president of the college in 1850.

Controversy surrounded Finney's work on several levels. He introduced into revivalism many "new measures" that shocked more conservative evangelists. His preaching style was popular and colloquial, though forceful and laced with the logic of the lawyer. He popularized the "protracted meeting" that continued for several days or weeks and employed the "anxious bench," a row of seats in the front of the church for those under "conviction" of sin. Perhaps the most controversial of his "new measures" was encouraging women to pray and speak in "promiscuous" or mixed assemblies.

But the content of Finney's preaching was as troubling to conservatives as his methods. Revivalism is generally understood in terms of the dramatic conversion of profligate sinners, but such an image is not true to the literal meaning of "revival." Finney's message was directed primarily to church people or "professors of religion" not living up to the fullness of Christian existence. The revival was a means of "breaking the power of the world and of sin over Christians." This involved the accusation that many (perhaps most) church people were less than vital Christians, a suggestion vigorously resisted by the traditional clergy. But this call to a "revived" Christian life incorporated the implicit demand that true conversion evidence itself in good works and commitment to the welfare of others. In such dynamics is the beginning of an impulse to reform activity.

Finney also generated controversy by his repudiation of "Old Calvinism" that discouraged human effort and created a certain "aristocracy of the elect." He vigorously denounced the old doctrine of election and denied that one must wait for the "miracle of conversion" that God would bring about according to divine discretion—or not at all. Finney argued that God wills that all should be converted and receives all who turn from their sin. This implied a new role for the human will and a new emphasis on human ability. When this doctrine was transposed into the social sphere, it meant that God had given men and women a role in the shaping of society and that nothing had to be accepted as it was.

Certain other features of Finney's thought moved him in the direction of egalitarianism. Finney affirmed not only that all may be saved but also that the fundamental fact about a person is human sin and the need of conversion. Lifting such convictions to determinative principles resulted in a profound "leveling" effect that produced a "Christian egalitarianism" congenial to the emerging Jacksonian affirmation of the value of the common person. Lyman Beecher, a more conservative revivalist from New England, disliked the democratic Western revivalists who implied that "all men, because sinners, are therefore to be treated alike by ministers of the gospel without respect to age or station in society." Here are the seeds of a very basic egalitarianism, which was later to bear fruit in abolitionism and feminism.

For Finney the essence of sin was selfishness. Such concern for one's own welfare was directly contradicted by God's character, especially the attribute of benevolence. To be "converted" for Finney was to forsake one's own interests for the sake of others. This reflection of God's benevolence in the life of the convert would evidence itself in "doing good" to all and becoming as "useful" as possible in the world. The natural outlet in Finney's time for such impulses was a series of "benevolent societies" set up for every conceivable philanthropy and social crusade. Finney's converts threw themselves into such work.

Finney himself made conversion central and was never willing to substitute reform for revival, but he did make the reforms an "appendage" to revival. In discussing the slavery issue, for example, the evangelist wished to make "abolition an appendage, just as we made temperance an appendage of the revival in Rochester." By this connection Finney preserved the centrality of revivals while still promoting reforms and propelling his converts into new positions on social issues.

This conjunction of reform and revival was also reversible. Finney argued not only that revivals should produce reforms but also that resistance to reform was one of the great "hindrances of revival." In his *Lectures on Revivals of Religion* Finney argued that "revivals are hindered when ministers and *churches take wrong ground in regard to any question involving human rights*." He applied this particularly to slavery, insisting that "the church cannot turn away from this question." He argued that "the silence of Christians upon the subject is virtually saying that they do not consider slavery as a sin" and claimed that "it is vain for the churches to resist for fear of destruction, contention, and strife" or to "account it an act of *piety* to turn away the ear from hearing this cry of distress" from the "shackled and bleeding" slaves.

Finney even argued that if the church fails to speak out on such an issue "she is perjured, and the Spirit of God departs from her." In effect, he insisted that the spiritual vitality of the church is sapped, not by her involvement in social questions, but rather by her failure to embrace reform. In Finney's own words, "One of the reasons for the low state of religion at the present time, is that many churches have taken the wrong side of the subject of slavery, have suffered prejudice to prevail over principle, and have feared to call this abomination by its true name." Finney went on to call for the use of church discipline on the *social* sin of "slaveholding." Since it is impossible for the church "to take a neutral ground on this subject," while she "tolerates slaveholders in her communion SHE JUSTIFIES THE PRACTICE." Though Finney refused to disrupt the church practices of others, he affirmed that "where I *have authority*, I exclude slaveholders from the [Lord's Supper], and I will as long as I live."

Finney, however, was not honored for such conviction by mid-twentieth-century evangelicals. Editions of his works from the 1950s and '60s were often expurgated. Offending passages were removed, leaving the impression that Finney avoided moral and ethical disputes for the sake of the "spiritual." V. Raymond Edman's book *Finney Lives On*, for example, contained a synopsis of the *Lectures on Revivals of Religion* listing only twenty-two of twenty-four "hindrances to revival" in the original edition. Omitted were references to "resistance to reform" and "taking the wrong ground on questions of human rights." The remaining "hindrances" were renumbered with no indication that Finney claimed that the spiritual vitality of the church may be destroyed from within by failure to take a stand on social issues.

But an even more egregious example of such censorship is found in *Revival Fire*.[4] This volume contains "letters on revivals" originally published in the *Oberlin Evangelist*. They represent Finney's mature thought and were written to deal with the emotional excitement that accompanied revivals and the failure of converts to continue in the Christian life. One of the most striking of the original letters was titled "The Pernicious Attitude of the Church on the Reforms of the Age." This title was retained in the mid-twentieth-century editions of *Revival Fire*, but the content of the letter that followed was entirely different! The letter printed treated the problem of "excitement."

The original text of that letter follows. Though lengthy, it is Finney's most stirring statement on the relationship of the church to reform. It had been completely excised from the twentieth-century editions of the letters and was available in only a very few surviving sets of the original *Oberlin Evangelist*.

Letters on Revivals—No. 23
By Prof. Finney
The Pernicious Attitude of the Church on the Reforms of the Age

To all the Friends and especially all the ministers of our Lord Jesus Christ:

Dear Brethren:

There is one subject upon which I must remark further, and yet I fear it will be impossible to do it justice without giving offense. One of the most serious impediments that have been thrown in the way of revivals of religion and one that has no doubt deeply grieved the Spirit of God is the fact that the church to a very great extent has lost sight of its own appropriate work and has left it in a great measure to be conducted by those who are for the most part illy prepared for the work. The work to which I refer is the reformation of mankind.

It is melancholy and amazing to see to what an extent the church treats the different branches of reform either with indifference, or

4. This book appeared in several twentieth-century editions. A 1970s reprint was in the Dimension Books paperback series published by Bethany Fellowship of Minneapolis.

with direct opposition. There is not, I venture to say upon the whole earth an inconsistency more monstrous, more God-dishonoring, and I must say more manifestly insane than the attitude which many of the churches take in respect to nearly every branch of reform which is needed among mankind.

To such an extent is this true that scarcely a church can be found in the land which as a body will have anything to do with reform. Hence the only way in which Christians in the churches who would do any thing towards reforming mankind can make their influence felt is by forming societies, composed often partly of Christians and partly of those who profess no religion. These unite together to concentrate their influence against some form of iniquity that is cursing mankind.

Now the great business of the church is to reform the world—to put away every kind of sin. The church of Christ was originally organized to be a body of reformers. The very profession of Christianity implies the profession and virtually an oath to do all that can be done for universal reformation of the world. The Christian church was designed to make aggressive movements in every direction—to lift up her voice and put forth her energies against iniquity in high and low places—to reform individuals, communities, and governments, and never rest until the kingdom and the greatness of the kingdom under the whole heaven shall be given to the people of the saints of the most High God—until every form of iniquity shall be driven from the earth.

Now when we consider the appropriate business of the church—the very end for which every Christian vows eternal consecration, and then behold her appalling inconsistencies everywhere apparent, I do not wonder that so many persons are led to avow the solemn conviction that the nominal church is apostate from God. When we consider the manner in which the movement in behalf of the slave has been treated by ecclesiastical bodies, by missionary associations, by churches, and ministers, throughout the land, is it any wonder that the Church is forsaken of the Spirit of God?

Look at the Moral Reform movement. A few devoted, self-denying females, engaged in a mighty conflict with the great sin of licentiousness. This struggle has been maintained for years; and yet how few comparatively of the churches as such have treated this effort in any other way than with contempt. A few devoted Christian women in various churches form societies to aid in this work; but where are the churches themselves as a body? Where are these sworn reformers—these men and women who profess to be waging everlasting war against every form of sin? Where are the ministry [clergy]? Do they lift up their voice like a trumpet? Do they cry aloud and spare not? Do they as John Adams says, thunder and lighten from their pulpits, every Sabbath against these sins?

It is amazing to see what excuses are made by ministers for remaining silent in respect to almost every branch of reform.

And pray what can be meant by the sickening cry of moral suasion? The church with a great many ministers have resorted to the plea of using moral suasion as the means of ridding the world of intemperance, licentiousness, slavery and every other legalized abomination; but pray what can be meant by moral suasion? Moral Government surely is a system of moral suasion. Moral suasion includes whatever is designed and adapted to influence the will of a moral agent.

Law, rewards, and punishments—these things and such as these are the very heart and soul of moral suasion. It would seem as if a great many people mean by moral suasion nothing more than flattery and palaver. Consequently when efforts are made to secure legislation that shall put these abominations away, they are afraid to employ government lest it could be a departure from the system of moral suasion. But is not God's government one of moral suasion? Are not his mighty judgments on the one hand and his mercies on the other, moral suasion?

But not to dwell on the subject of moral suasion; the idea I wish to present to the brethren is this—the great sin and utter shame of the Church and of so many of the ministry [clergy] in neglecting or refusing to speak out and act promptly and efficiently on these great questions of reform. How could they more directly grieve and quench the Spirit of God than by such a course? Abandon the great work to which they are pledged and sworn, and yet profess to be Christians! No wonder that such a ministry should look coldly on revivals and find it impossible to promote them. After so much light has blazed before the churches on these subjects, it cannot be that they resist or neglect without great sin.

And shall it be persevered in? If so there can be no doubt that revivals must utterly cease—that the Spirit of God will be grieved entirely away from the ministry and the churches, and nothing better can be expected than utter and universal desolation.

Believe me, dear brethren, it grieves me greatly to feel constrained to speak thus. Is it not a shame; are we not ashamed and shall we not blush to see the Church of God not only turn back from reforming the world—refusing to lead in reform as she ought to do, and then turn round and oppose others who are compelled to lead for want of help and countenance of those who ought to go forward in these enterprises? If doctors of divinity—if ecclesiastical bodies, theological seminaries and colleges would but lead on in these enterprises, God forbid that they should not have their place. If they would but go forward the Church would follow them, and many who are now compelled to lead because these refuse, would rejoice to fall in behind and sustain them with all their might.

But if the church will not lead—if doctors of divinity, ecclesiastical bodies, colleges and seminaries will do nothing but get together to pass resolutions condemning the movements of reform, what shall be done? Shall they refuse to work in these departments and also hinder those who would work? Who pretends that so great wisdom has been manifested in the various branches of reform as might have been, had the spiritual leaders only taken the right position? What can be expected but error and confusion, while nearly all the spiritual influence in the world is brought to oppose instead of promote reforms? My brethren, if ecclesiastical bodies, colleges, and seminaries will only go forward—who will not bid them God speed? But if they will not go forward—if we hear little or nothing from them but complaint, denunciation, and rebuke in respect to almost every branch of reform, what can be done?

My soul is sick and agonized with such a state of things. The position of the Church is one of the greatest wonders of the world;—and yet we are gravely asking, why we do not have revivals of religion? Why has the Spirit of God forsaken us? and many are even glad to have revivals cease, and seem to be disposed to quell every thing down into a state of death-like apathy on every branch of reform.

Now until the Church shall arise and take a different attitude, I am confident that nothing else can be expected than a retrograde movement on the part of the Churches until not even a form of godliness remains among them.

Why cannot we all do in respect to reforms as Pres. Edwards did in respect to revivals? He fearlessly pointed out whatever was wrong and of evil tendency in the means used to promote them, and at the same time was careful to show a more excellent way. His opposition to what was wrong, although fearless and uncompromising, was never so prominent as to overshadow all his engagedness in promoting them.

He was their powerful, zealous, and successful advocate and promoter. It became him then to speak out and rebuke whatever was wrong. Every body saw that his rebukes arose not from opposition to revivals as such, but to his great love for them and from a quenchless zeal to promote them. When he lifted his admonitory voice, the friends of revivals would listen because they knew it to be the voice of a friend and not an enemy of revivals. Everybody knew he spake of the evils sometimes connected with revivals because he loved them in their purity.

Now why cannot we all do so on the subject of reform? My brethren, let us all come forward and show ourselves to be reformers—put our heads and hearts together to promote every branch of reform and also revivals of religion, and then we shall hold a position in which we can successfully oppose and correct the errors of the day either in revivals or reforms. But who will listen to ministers, ecclesiastical bodies, doctors of divinity, missionary societies, or any body else who make no aggressive movements at all in respect to any reform and say almost nothing except to rebuke and condemn? They can talk eloquently of the evils incident to revivals, but are not like Pres. Edwards, zealous and successful in promoting them themselves. They can denounce the madness of abolitionists and the errors and extravagances of both the leaders and followers in other reforms; but alas, how few of them have any thing efficient or impressive to say to promote these great objects either by encouragement, instruction or counsel.

Now if ecclesiastical bodies generally, doctors of divinity, colleges and theological seminaries, had uniformly manifested zeal in all departments of reform, they would be heard. If ministers had manifested zeal and efficiency in these reforms, their churches would hear and respect them, and the ministry might lead them anywhere. But now the ministers are complaining that their churches are divided—that themselves are losing the confidence of their people—that ministerial influence is becoming paralyzed—and church influence an abomination.

Is it possible, my dearly beloved brethren, that we can remain blind to the tendencies of things—to the causes that are operating to produce alienation, division, distrust, to grieve away the Spirit, overthrow revivals, and cover the land with darkness and the shadow of death? Is it not time for us, brethren, to repent, to be candid and search out wherein we have been wrong and publicly and privately confess it, and pass public resolutions in our general ecclesiastical bodies, recanting and confessing what has been wrong—confessing in our pulpits, through the press, and in every proper way our sins as Christians and as ministers—our want of sympathy with Christ, our want of compassion for the slave, for the inebriate, for the wretched prostitute, and for all the miserable and ignorant of the earth.

    May the Lord have mercy on us, my brethren

    Your brother, C. G. Finney

Postscript by Douglas M. Strong

Charles Finney's insistence that, in order to be effective, revivals must be accompanied by social reform—especially reform related to "any question involving human rights"—led him to give his encouragement to a host of antislavery activities. Eventually, he even supported the initiative by a faction of abolitionists in the 1840s to move toward direct political action, a surprising turn for Finney, given his general suspicion of politics.

Earlier, in the 1830s, along with most evangelical reformers, Finney advocated antislavery measures by using the strategy of "moral suasion," that is, convincing converted individuals to oppose slavery by ethical arguments and then expecting that the aggregate of many such persuaded individuals would sway public opinion against slaveholding. By 1839, however, a number of abolitionist agitators—including many who were evangelicals—became frustrated with the perceived slowness and inefficacy of this method. They advanced a strategy in which they would nominate and then (hopefully) elect candidates to public office who pledged to enact antislavery legislation. After a few independent nominations for local offices, these politically minded antislavery leaders decided to form a political party—the Liberty Party—that would present a slate of candidates for state offices, Congress, and even the presidency. This avowedly Christian abolitionist party fielded candidates throughout the 1840s and functioned as a third alternative and foil to the establishment Whig and Democratic parties. (In the election of 1844, the Liberty presidential candidate, James G. Birney, took enough votes away from Whig candidate Henry Clay in heavily antislavery upstate New York to throw New York's electoral votes to the Democratic candidate, James K. Polk, thereby allowing Polk to win the White House.)

Since Finney believed that "Christians were bound to reform human governments," he gave his blessing to the Liberty Party cause, his first and only entrée into political advocacy. As a measure of his patronage, Finney offered the use of his distinctive "big tent" to hold the national nominating convention of the Liberty Party in 1843. This famous canopy had been employed for revival services throughout the northern states, accommodating three thousand people at a time, and so the Liberty Party's appropriation of Finney's tent indicated to Christian voters a combination of antislavery electioneering with evangelical zeal. The big tent also serves as a fitting image for the type of conversion-based evangelical social reform characteristic of the nineteenth century.

Within a few years, Finney feared that too much political activity on the part of sanctified Christians was deflecting attention away from the essential task of evangelism. He warned ministers who preached on political topics not to forget "to make the conversion of sinners, and the

sanctification of the church the great end at which they aim— always insisting that right political action will follow . . . from a right state of heart." As before, Finney asserted that regeneration would necessarily elicit ethically minded political action. He continued to vote for antislavery candidates but

Finney's Big Tent: used for revival meetings and the 1843 Liberty Party nominating convention

ceased his active campaigning on behalf of political abolitionism. Many of Finney's followers, though, had none of his caution or reluctance regarding the mixing of evangelical faith and political action (as described further in chap. 7). They continued to promote the Liberty Party as a Christian means of effecting the "government of God" in America.

In a 2012 book of essays, famed author Marilynne Robinson wrote at length about the significance of Oberlin, Finney, and his colleagues. She expounded about Oberlin because she modeled the fictional town of Gilead (in her Pulitzer Prize–winning novel of the same name) after an Oberlin-like community. She expounded about Finney because she was frustrated with other writers who too facilely tried to make Finney out to be an aggressive fundamentalist or charlatan—who, because Finney was a revivalist, assumed that he must also have been a conservative purveyor of religious excesses and eccentricities. In contrast, Robinson forthrightly stated that "Charles Finney was a great reformer. His two signature causes were the abolition of slavery and the enhancement of women. It is an anachronism to call him a fundamentalist." He came to Oberlin, Robinson wrote, "which was then . . . in a great swamp in a mud hole, to help create a little society organized around the equality of classes, races, and genders."

Robinson wanted her readers to know about Finney because "we have no equivalent figure now, though during his lifetime there were many revivalists who were also educators, highly cultured men committed to radical social reform." She continues: "It would be difficult indeed to reckon the debt we owe them, both as individuals and as a culture, and just as difficult to imagine what America might have become, or remained, without their efforts and their influence. . . . Perhaps the only modern figure it would be meaningful to compare with Finney is another preacher and reformer, Martin Luther King, Jr."[5]

---

5. Marilynne Robinson, "Who Was Oberlin?," in *When I Was a Child I Read Books* (New York: Farrar, Straus & Giroux, 2012), 165–81.

3

Theodore Weld

Evangelical Reformer

Amerian church historian William Warren Sweet has claimed that "perhaps the chief significance of Charles G. Finney lies not so much in the fact that he was the instrument in adding tens of thousands to the active ranks of the American churches, as in the circumstance that these new converts became active participants in every forward movement of their time."[1] To whichever fact one attributes Finney's "chief significance," his revivals certainly raised up an army of young converts who became the troops of the reform movements of his age. The antislavery forces in particular were drawn largely from the converts of Finney's revivals.

Probably the most important of these antislavery workers was Theodore Weld, converted under the ministry of Finney and for a while the evangelist's assistant. Weld devoted the whole of his life

---

1. William Warren Sweet, *Revivalism in America: Its Origin, Growth, and Decline* (New York: Charles Scribner's Sons, 1945), 160.

to reform and the antislavery struggle. According to the *Dictionary of American Biography*, "Weld was not only the greatest of the

Theodore D. Weld: abolitionist reformer converted under Finney's ministry

abolitionists; he was also one of the greatest figures of his time." Yet Weld was nearly lost to history, and it is only by a strange twist of events that we know as much about him as we do.

By natural modesty and firm convictions Weld resisted all efforts to thrust him into prominence. He declined the professorship of theology at Oberlin, insisting that it go to Finney, and the executive secretaryship of the American Anti-Slavery Society, arguing that his work was in the ranks.

He refused invitations to speak at antislavery conventions because he "loathed" such "ostentatious display" and feared the "habit of gadding" from one convention to another. Weld would not let his speeches and letters be printed and published his books anonymously. He shunned the press and worked in the "West" (especially Ohio) away from the Eastern centers of influence. He chose, moreover, the obscurity of working in small towns "among the yeomanry," self-consciously arguing that "the great cities . . . must be burned down by *back fires*. The springs to touch . . . lie in the country."

Weld is consequently little represented in the sources historians use, and most interpretations of the antislavery movement focus on Boston and William Lloyd Garrison, editor of the *Liberator*. Such history naturally emphasizes liberal and Unitarian aspects of the movement and neglects the extent to which even Garrison was a product of revivalistic evangelicalism. Garrison, moreover, was somewhat erratic and anticlerical and often more of a liability than an asset to the cause as it tried to permeate the Midwest and the church. Interpretations centering on Boston and Garrison, therefore, had difficulty explaining how antislavery sentiment became dominant throughout the North before the Civil War.

This New England and Garrisonian perspective was challenged in the 1930s by economist Gilbert Barnes of Ohio Wesleyan University, who began to track down elusive references to Weld. Through Weld's grandson, Barnes finally located in an old farmhouse a trunk of letters that enabled him to offer a new interpretation of the abolitionist movement that emphasized its revivalistic origins. Barnes argued that "the agitation was accomplished not so much by heroes of reform as by very numerous obscure persons, prompted by an impulse religious in character and evangelical in spirit, which began in the Great Revival in 1830, was translated for a time into anti-slavery organization, and then broadened into a Congressional movement against slavery and the south."[2]

The validity of Barnes's thesis is still debated, but studies in the 1970s of abolitionism assume to great extent his perspective. The least that can be said is that revivalism (especially that of Finney) was a major force behind the pre–Civil War crusade against slavery. Barnes's work also brought to the fore a remarkable person all too long neglected: Theodore Weld, the greatest of the evangelical abolitionists and reformers.

Weld was born in 1803 into a Connecticut minister's home that traced its ancestry through a long line of distinguished New England clergymen and theologians. A failure of eyesight during his studies at Phillips Academy caused Weld to drop out of school and take up lecturing on mnemonics—the art of memory improvement. After three years of astonishing success on the lecture platform (developing skills later to be put to other purposes), Weld returned to school at Hamilton College near Utica, New York.

Shortly thereafter Weld was called to Utica by the death of an uncle. Evangelist Charles G. Finney was in the area, and Weld's aunt tried to get her nephew to attend the revival meetings. Having already

2. Gilbert H. Barnes and Dwight L. Dumond, *Letters of Theodore Dwight Weld, Angelina Grimké Weld, and Sarah Grimké, 1822–1844* (Gloucester, MA: Peter Smith, 1965), 1:xvi–xvii.

gained a reputation for ridiculing Finney, Weld declined, but finally agreed to attend a service at which another preacher was supposedly scheduled to speak. Once he was seated, his aunt and several other ladies filled up the pew. Weld attempted to leave when Finney arose to preach, but the ladies fell to their knees in prayer and pressed their heads against the pew in front blocking his only means of exit.

Theodore Weld resigned himself to his fate of listening to the evangelist. But Finney, tipped off in advance to Weld's presence, preached on the text "one sinner destroyeth much good." Weld later reported that "for an hour, he just held me up on his toasting fork before that audience." Meeting Finney the next day in a store, Weld vented his disgust in "all the vocabulary of abuse the language afforded." Later ashamed of his actions, Weld sought out Finney to apologize, but before he could start, they embraced and fell to the floor, "sobbing and praying, sobbing and praying."

From this moment Weld was a disciple of Finney. He worked for a while in the "holy band" composed of Finney's assistants. In that work Weld was a major force in pushing Finney toward one of his controversial "new measures"—that of allowing women to speak in "promiscuous" or mixed assemblies. This foreshadowed the later practice of women taking to the platform in defense of abolitionism and the consequent birth of feminism. A dozen years later Weld married one of the most prominent feminists and antislavery agitators of the era, Angelina Grimké. Weld claimed at that time that he had affirmed since he was a boy "that there is no reason why *woman* should not make laws, administer justice, sit in the chair of state, plead at the bar or in the pulpit, if she has the qualifications." Weld also broke the conventions of his day by suggesting that women should feel free to initiate courtship.

Weld soon moved into other reforms to which Finney's revivalism gave impetus. Under the influence of Charles Stuart, another member of Finney's "holy band," Weld moved toward an antislavery position. He also regularly lectured on the question of temperance, marshaling for the cause a vast array of statistics and powerful rhetoric. In 1831 Weld became the general agent of the Society for Promoting Manual Labor in Literary Institutions. In this work he became an early

advocate of a theme that permeated many institutions founded in the
wake of Finney's revivals. This society encouraged several hours of
manual labor each day, primarily out of concern for physical fitness,
but the practice also permitted indigent students to earn their way
through school. This was an early manifestation of a concern for total
education and an antecedent of physical education.

But the antislavery struggle increasingly absorbed Weld's attention.
At first he advocated colonization, but travels in the South and contacts
with the emerging school of "immediate abolitionism" pushed him
in a new direction. Weld urged his financial supporters in New York
(primarily the Tappan brothers, see chap. 6) to join the antislavery
struggle and to throw their resources behind it. These discussions
climaxed in the founding in 1833 of the American Anti-Slavery Society.
This organization then launched a major attack on colonization, and
Finney himself signed the first letter of challenge to the Colonization
Society demanding to know if they supported the "complete extinc-
tion of slavery in the United States."

In the midst of these discussions Weld enrolled in Lane Theological
Seminary in Cincinnati and became embroiled in the abolitionist debates that led to the "Lane Rebellion" and the founding of Oberlin
College. (These events are narrated in chap. 4.) While in Cincinnati
he spent every spare moment in the black community. In a survey
of the three thousand blacks in Cincinnati, he discovered that more
than three-fourths had recently bought their freedom and half still
had members of their family in bondage. The suffering and gruel-
ing work to which these freedmen were subjected in attempting to
scrape together funds to purchase the freedom of their relatives was
more than Weld could stand. "After spending three or four hours, and
getting facts, I was forced to stop from sheer heartache and agony."

Weld's identification with the black community was profound and
belies the common accusation that abolitionists were nonetheless
racially prejudiced.

> If I ate in the City it was at their tables. If I slept in the City it was
> in their homes. If I attended parties, it was *theirs—weddings—
> theirs—Funerals—theirs—Religious meetings—theirs—Sabbath*

schools—Bible Classes—theirs. During the 18 months that I spent at Lane seminary *I did not attend Dr. Beecher's Church once*. Nor did I attend any other of the Presbyterian Churches in the City except brother Mahan's, . . . I was with the colored people in their meetings by day and by night.

After leaving Lane, Weld accepted an assignment as an agent for the newly founded American Anti-Slavery Society. In this work his experience and abilities found fullest expression. Testimonies left behind by his hearers indicate that he was a powerful and striking orator. Testifying to his "rare combination of talents," James G. Birney, also a prominent abolitionist, predicted, "I give him one year to abolitionize Ohio."

One key to Weld's impact was his adaption of the techniques of revivalism—especially the "protracted meeting" and the "call to decision"—to the antislavery cause. Weld would start by lecturing in the Presbyterian church in each town, but the first night's lecture would often incite a riot, forcing him to seek other quarters. After a day or two, the resistance would break, and Weld would leave behind some new "converts" to found a local chapter of the American Anti-Slavery Society. Weld started his work in Ohio in October 1834. In May 1835, the national organization had 38 local chapters in Ohio (out of a total of 220). A year later the chapters totaled 527, but 133 were in Ohio.

Impressed with Weld's success, the national committee sent out seventy such agents as Jesus had sent out seventy disciples to preach. Weld and Henry B. Stanton (author, Lane Rebel, and later husband of feminist Elizabeth Cady Stanton) were called to New York to train this famous group of "Seventy"—over one-third of whom came out of the abolition struggle at Lane that Weld had ignited. By this means Weld multiplied his influence and played a major role in spreading the abolitionist gospel across the country.

Unfortunately Weld lost his voice about this time and retired from lecturing to work behind the scenes editing and writing. His first task was to produce in book form the "Bible Argument against Slavery" that he had developed and in the use of which he had instructed the Seventy. Though published anonymously, this book immediately went through several editions and became a major tool of the antislavery movement.

Soon after this, Weld first declared his long-concealed love for Angelina Grimké, one of the Seventy. This mutual affection, long sacrificed to the needs of reform movement, now found culmination in an 1838 wedding. Committed to simplicity of life, the newly married couple had difficulty outfitting their home with furniture that was not "tricked out and covered with carved wood or bedizoned and gew gawed and gilded and tipt off with variegated colors." The wedding cake was prepared by a black confectioner who used nothing but "free sugar." ("Free sugar" was produced by freedmen rather than slaves—the economic boycott was freely used in the struggle against slavery.) The wedding ceremony was a simple exchange of vows in which Weld renounced the rights to Angelina's person and property granted him by the "sexist" laws of the age. Prayer was offered by both black and white clergymen. Soon thereafter Angelina was excommunicated by her Quaker society for marrying outside the sect.

Weld's next project was another book, *Slavery As It Is*. He combed Southern newspapers for evidence of the cruelty of slavery (such as ads seeking the return of runaway slaves identified by scars or other signs of mistreatment). These were compiled by Weld, Angelina, and her sister Sarah into a devastating critique of slavery that sold more than one hundred thousand copies in the first year. This book was a major influence on Harriet Beecher Stowe, author of *Uncle Tom's Cabin*, who reported that she had been profoundly influenced by the debates on slavery Weld had initiated at Lane Seminary while her father had been president of the school. Mrs. Stowe claimed that she had slept with *Slavery As It Is* under her pillow while writing her novel.

Such research and propaganda prepared Weld for the next step in the struggle. In the early 1840s he was called to Washington to do research for John Quincy Adams, who was leading the antislavery struggle in Congress. While in Washington Weld usually attended the churches of his black friends. Those services were noisier than he would have liked, but he much preferred them to the white churches in Washington, whose religion seemed a sham put on for the sake of reputation and appearance.

Weld had become increasingly alienated from the churches of the era, and after leaving Washington he rejected the suggestion of Lewis Tappan that he take a church in New York City. Weld granted some exceptions, but his impression of the ministry from his years in the antislavery struggle was that

> there is among the professed ministers of Christ such connivance at cherished sin, such truckling subserviency to power, such clinging with mendicant sycophancy to the skirts of wealth and influence, such humoring of pampered lusts, such cowering before bold transgression when it stalks among the high places of power with fashion in its train, or to sum up all, such floating in the wake of an unholy public sentiment, instead of beating back its waves with a "thus saith the Lord" and a "thou art the man"—that even men of the world who are shrewd discerners, regard them rather as the obsequious cooks and confectioners who cater for a capricious palate, than as the faithful physician who administers the medicine demanded by the disease, however much the patient may loathe it, and steadily pushes the probe to the core, whatever his struggles or upbraidings.

After service in Washington Weld retired to farming and teaching, though his work was often interrupted for antislavery activities. A superb teacher, he was entrusted with the children of many abolitionists who sought the particular mixture of modern techniques and moral education that Weld offered. Engaged in these and related activities, Weld lived to the age of ninety-one, dying in 1895.

The letters that Weld and the Grimké sisters left behind are a delight to read. Addressing themselves to issues that still bedevil the evangelical world, these letters often offer startlingly pertinent advice.

They belie, for example, the common assumption that the abolitionists were concerned primarily with ridding themselves of complicity in the sin of slavery rather than the welfare of the slaves. They demonstrate that the Christian egalitarianism behind revivalist abolitionism understood the issues to be prejudice and caste as well as slavery. There was no sign of racial prejudice in Weld, who insisted that "persons are to be treated according to their intrinsic worth irrespective of Color, shape, condition, or what not." Weld's was a persistent voice calling the American Anti-Slavery Society to greater consistency. As Angelina wrote to Weld before their marriage: "I rejoice that you continue to identify yourself with our colored friends—to board with them, etc. I am sure that the poor and oppressed both *white* and black can never be benefited without mingling with them on terms of equality."

This egalitarianism was carried over into their marriage, and Theodore and Angelina struggled continually with the problems of relating feminist convictions to their lives. Weld had been warned that a feminist like Angelina would be only "an obtrusive noisy clamorer" in the "domestic circle" and that it was "*impossible* for a man of high and pure feeling ever to *marry*" her—that "nature recoiled at it." Weld was convinced that "the devil of dominion over women will be one of the last that will be cast out" of men and worried about his ability to put his convictions into practice. But they were both convinced that their views freed them for a higher and deeper relationship that transcended the conventional patterns of male dominance and feminine wiles.

No one can doubt the profoundly Christian convictions that lay behind their lives. This is most poignant in love letters that reveal struggle with Christian commitment and its relationship to human commitments of love. Weld wondered to Angelina, "Do I love my blessed savior *less* because I *love you* as I do?" His own answer was that "My love for you has quickened me in love and gratitude . . . and in a more near and tender communion with him who loved us and died for us." In a similar way they were concerned that their marriage not hinder their effectiveness in the reforms to which they were committed—and to which they felt divinely called.

Something of the character of that Christian commitment is revealed in a very interesting sidelight. Their day, like our own, was troubled with arcane speculation about the end times. Angelina, in particular, became agitated with the prophecies of William Miller, whose predictions about the return of Christ placed the date in the midst of her pregnancy. Weld's response to Angelina was that

> the study of prophecy has cast great witchery over minds of a certain cast. It powerfully stimulates curiosity, love of the marvelous,

the element of superstition . . . the desire for novelty, etc. . . . I do not contend that prophecy is never to be studied, but that *God* is *first* to be studied, and so studied and communed with as to have the soul taken into captivity, moulded, filled with him; its principles, its taste, its tendencies, its habits, its intensities so incorporated with the mind of Christ . . . as to secure that subjection and allegiance and vital union with him which ushers into fullness of God.

Such convictions little prepare us for a later spiritual and theological struggle that led to a transformation of their faith. Despairing of the "profitless forms and dead formality and timid time serving of the church and the ministry as a body," they turned increasingly toward the "practicalities" of faith known "experimentally." This involved moving from church forms and doctrinal structures to a simple "loving and following Jesus" that climaxed in Unitarianism.

What was involved in this pilgrimage is not entirely clear. Weld's biographers have not given careful attention to this period and are not attuned to the questions we would ask. Weld reflects a deeply biblical and committed faith pitted against the churches of the time. He and Angelina shared the alienation of the abolitionists during the 1840s as traditional churches refused to embrace reform. This disaffection was clearly related to the revivalists' alienation from the churches, and was therefore "unorthodox" primarily in the sense that it failed to follow patterns of traditional church life. How much more was involved is not certain. The letters exist for a study that not only would illumine the pre–Civil War era but would also show how the failure of the church to embrace the great moral concerns of an age can drive out sensitive youth who will find moral leadership in other circles.

4

The Lane Rebellion
and the Founding
of Oberlin College

The major institution founded to perpetuate both the revivalism and the social position of Charles G. Finney was Oberlin College. At Oberlin Jonathan Blanchard gave his address titled the "State of the Perfect Society." Blanchard longed to teach at Oberlin, though he was unable to accept the invitation when it finally came. Many of today's Christian colleges were founded to be "little Oberlins." But Oberlin was not just another Christian college; it was hated in its time as a hotbed of radicalism. Socially, its major contribution was to the antislavery struggle. As Finney commented toward the end of the Civil War, "The fact is that Oberlin turned the scale in all of the Northwest" [the term used for what we now refer to as the upper Midwest]. But Oberlin and its supporters also made major contributions to feminism, the peace movement, the doctrine of civil disobedience, temperance, and other reforms of the era.

It is difficult to know where to begin the story of Oberlin. Its prehistory is as fascinating as its history. One place to start is with Theodore

Weld's decision to join the first class to enter Lane Theological Seminary in Cincinnati. Just as Weld was moving toward immediate abolitionism, this seminary was founded to reach the West with the spirit of revivalism and reform. Lyman Beecher, now somewhat reconciled to Finney and his ideals, had taken the presidency in part at the urging of Finney. Beecher's brand of reform was more moderate and "polite." On the slavery issue he was committed to gradual abolition and colonization, but Lane did admit blacks (becoming one of the first institutions in America to drop the color line) and faced opposition for positions it did take.

Lane's first theological class consisted of about forty students. Of these, Theodore Weld was the only forthright abolitionist. One student later described "a general consent in the institution that slavery was somehow wrong and to be got rid of" but "not a readiness to pronounce it a sin." Part of Weld's motive in going to Lane was "to introduce anti-slavery sentiments, and have the whole subject thoroughly discussed." He succeeded.

Weld worked quietly to convert members of the campus colonization society to abolitionism. By the spring of 1834 he had convinced enough to challenge the rest to an eighteen-day debate on the two positions. At the conclusion the students voted almost unanimously in favor of immediate abolitionism and, following the dictates of sound strategy, they proceeded to organize an abolition society whose officers were all Southerners. Believing that "faith without works is dead," the students put their faith into practice by forming a "large and efficient organization for elevating the colored people of Cincinnati." This included literacy classes, lectures on academic subjects, Sunday schools, Bible classes, and research on the financial and social problems of Cincinnati's three thousand blacks. But most offensive was the students' insistence on treating blacks as social equals, eating in their homes, staying overnight with them, and even allowing themselves to be seen on the streets with young black women. This was too much for the townspeople, who openly threatened mob actions to get rid of the school. Beecher and the faculty warned the students of the dangerous consequences of "carrying the doctrine of intercourse into practical effect."

The board of trustees, mostly solid Cincinnati businessmen operating in the South, finally took action. In a special meeting called over the

summer they insisted that "education must be completed before the
young are fitted to engage in the
collisions of active life," forbade
even the discussion of such issues
as slavery, and fired Professor John
Morgan, the only faculty member
who had sided with the students.
A later meeting confirmed these

*Lane Theological Seminary, Cincinnati,
Ohio: site of the "Lane Rebellion" of
Abolitionist students*

actions, arguing that "the location of the seminary . . . calls for some
peculiar cautionary measures" for fear that the "prosperity of the Institution will be much retarded and its usefulness generally diminished."
The *Cincinnati Journal* editorially supported the board with the comment that "a school, to prepare pious youth for preaching the gospel,
has not legitimate place" for such concerns as abolitionism.

But for the students, the issue was moral integrity and principle.
They raised the matter of freedom of speech, declaring that "free discussion being a duty is consequently a right, and as such, is inherent
and inalienable." At least forty students withdrew from the school
in protest. Most of these moved across town and set up an informal
"free seminary" at which they instructed themselves in theology and
continued their work among the blacks of Cincinnati.

Meanwhile, in another part of Ohio, another project was developing—also deeply influenced by Finney. John J. Shipherd and Philo P.
Stewart were founding a colony and a school, Christian in character
and abolitionist in conviction. Those who joined this community
pledged themselves to a particular lifestyle expressive of their understanding of the Christian faith. The "Oberlin Covenant" contains
twelve items, but since it epitomized the self-understanding of Oberlin and contains so many themes echoed in current discussions, it is
reproduced here in its entirety:

    1. Providence permitting, we engage as soon as practicable to
        remove to the Oberlin Colony, in Russia, Lorain County, Ohio,
        and there to fix our residence, for the express purpose of glorify-
        ing God in doing good to men to the extent of our ability.

2. We will hold and manage our estates personally, but pledge as perfect a community of interest as though we held a community of property.

3. We will hold in possession no more property than we believe that we can profitably manage for God, as His faithful stewards.

4. We will, by industry, economy, and Christian self-denial, obtain as much as we can, above our necessary personal or family expenses, and faithfully appropriate the same for the spread of the Gospel.

5. That we may have time and health for the Lord's service, we will eat only plain and wholesome food, renouncing all bad habits, and especially the smoking and chewing of tobacco, unless it is necessary as a medicine, and deny ourselves all strong and unnecessary drinks, even tea and coffee, as far as practicable, and everything expensive, that is simply calculated to gratify the palate.

6. That we may add to our time and health money for the service of the Lord, we renounce all the world's expensive and unwholesome fashions of dress, particularly tight dressing and ornamental attire.

7. And yet more to increase our means of serving Him who bought us with His blood, we will observe plainness and durability in the construction of our houses, furniture, carriages, and all that appertains to us.

8. We will strive continually to show that we, as the body of Christ, are members one of another; and will, while living, provide for the widows, orphans, and families of the sick and needy, as for ourselves.

9. We will take special pains to educate our children thoroughly, and to train them up, in body, intellect, and heart, for the service of the Lord.

10. We will feel that the interests of the Oberlin Institute are identified with ours, and do what we can to extend its influence to our fallen race.

11. We will make special efforts to sustain the institutions of the gospel at home and among our neighbors.

12. We will strive to maintain deep-toned and elevated personal piety, to "provoke each other to love and good works," to live together in all things as brethren, and to glorify God in our bodies and spirits, which are His.

But by 1834 Oberlin Institute was in desperate financial straits, and Shipherd was sent East to look for funds and a president for the struggling school. One report indicates that in a preparatory session of prayer and fasting Shipherd received the definite, but inexplicable, impression that he should go East by way of Cincinnati! There he visited Asa Mahan, the major defender of the Lane Seminary students among the members of Lane's board of trustees. (Mahan was pastor of the only Presbyterian church in the city that Weld had found interested in the slaves and blacks and the same church that Jonathan Blanchard was later to pastor.) Immediately there opened up the opportunity to gain for Oberlin a new president (Asa Mahan), an outstanding and popular faculty member (John Morgan—fired for his identification with the Lane Rebels), a sizable theological department of mature students, as well as the financial backing of Arthur Tappan, the New York businessman providing funds for the "free seminary."

But Mahan, Morgan, and the Lane Rebels would come only on condition that absolute freedom of speech be guaranteed on all reform issues and that blacks be admitted with whites. Shaken by the events at Lane, Oberlin trustees were at first reluctant but finally accepted a compromise. Finney agreed to come as professor of theology if the trustees would leave the matter of the admission of blacks in the hands of the faculty. With Mahan, Morgan, and Finney on the faculty, that decision was never in question. This compromise permitted the confluence of the radical abolitionism of the Lane Rebels and the communitarian and lifestyle-oriented radicalism of the Oberlin Colony. The foundations were laid for the emergence of the distinctive Christian radicalism of Oberlin College.

By the time the new school was announced, Oberlin had become the last refuge for radical students. All over the country conservative interests had suppressed antislavery societies and purged campuses of abolitionists. Nearly three hundred students poured into Oberlin the first year, and more the next—many more than Oberlin could physically accommodate. Immediately, too, opposition surfaced. One observer insisted that "Oberlin had before enemies enough for one Semny. Now they will increase ten fold." And Shipherd discovered that "Finneyism, Abolitionism, *etc*. are excuses of multitudes for not giving funds." But Shipherd and Oberlin believed that "public Institutions no less than

private Christians must do right however contrary to popular sentiment." On this great principle Oberlin College was launched.

"Oberlinism" was a complex ideology. The institution was first
and foremost a Christian college. Finney insisted that Oberlin "make
the conversion of sinners and the sanctification of Christians the
paramount work and subordinate to this all the educational opera-
tions." College life was intensely religious with frequent periods of

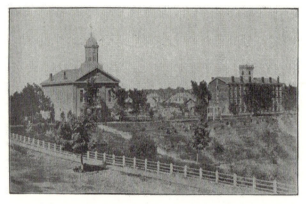

Oberlin College in 1850: view of Finney Chapel and Tappan Hall

revival. Students and faculty alike regularly conducted revival meetings
during vacations. Missions was also a dominant concern. By 1836
the campus had six different missionary societies, and in 1838 this
missionary impulse began to focus on the American Indian. (Oberlin
was concerned with more than missions to the Indian and opposed
government efforts at relocation and other violations of treaties.)

But Oberlin would have nothing to do with Christian faith unre-
lated to reform and boasted that "Oberlin College has been greatly
successful in making her students intelligent and vigorous reformers."
President Mahan insisted that "the fundamental spirit and aim of
Christianity is the correction of all abuses, a universal conformity to
the laws of our own existence as far as revealed to the mind, and a
quenchless thirst for knowledge on all subjects pertaining to the duties
and interest of humanity." At the same time Oberlin prided itself on
hearing all sides of any issue, avoiding personal denunciation in a spirit

of love for the oppressor as well as the oppressed, and maintaining a stance of "universal reform" rather than "fanatical" or "ultraistic" commitment to a single cause.

Oberlin's great issue was the antislavery struggle. Soon after the students arrived, they founded the Oberlin Anti-Slavery Society, whose two hundred members pledged to work for the "immediate emancipation of the whole colored race." Oberlin provided at least sixteen of the famous Seventy sent out as agents of the American Anti-Slavery Society (and more were Lane Rebels who did not move on to Oberlin). As was common in such work, these lecturers and organizers endured mob violence and other forms of abuse. Oberlinites were prominent in state and national antislavery organizations. Sermons and lectures on campus regularly returned to this theme. Convictions were so strong that residents of Oberlin found July 4 a "cruel mockery" (since it celebrated only the freedom of the white race) and preferred instead to honor August 1 (the anniversary of emancipation in the British West Indies). Nor did such concerns stop upon graduation. Oberlin alumni fanned out over the country to work among members of the black race, especially by founding schools.

Oberlin wished to make the whole Christian church an "antislavery society." The means was "moral suasion" or the use of Finney's "new measure revival techniques." The Oberlin Church passed a resolution that "as Slavery is a Sin no person shall be invited to preach or Minister to this church, or any Br. be invited to commune who is a slaveholder." The wider Congregational association of which Oberlin was a part declared that "*oppression* in all its forms is sin" and vowed to have "no Christian communion with those who practice slavery, nor with any who justify the system." When church agencies, such as missionary societies, refused to make abolitionism a firm plank in their policy statements, Oberlinites worked for the establishing of separate antislavery mission boards.

The peace movement also found support at Oberlin. Here, though, opinion was not uniform. First into the fray in 1840 was the Oberlin Non-Resistance Society, which renounced all use of force. More typical was the Oberlin Peace Society, founded in 1843. This group allowed that war might in some cases be just—though it took several weeks of debate to establish this position. But this conclusion was not used to avoid intense peace activity through writing, lecturing, education, and conferences. Nor did Oberlin hesitate to dissent from American war policy. The *Oberlin Evangelist* attacked President Polk for risking war with Britain through his "expansionist" policy of demanding all of the Oregon territory. The Mexican War provoked this response: "Wars of aggression like this we not only deprecate and deplore, but most unqualifiedly condemn. The conscience of the world and the court of heaven are against us." A year later the same war was described as "most dishonorable, unjust, and nefarious . . . conceived in sin."

Oberlin also made contributions to the women's movement, though it resisted the style of the "woman's rights" crusade. It was the first coeducational college in the world, a step that met much resistance. (Even reformer Lyman Beecher said that "this amalgamation of the sexes won't do. If you live in a Powder House, you blow up once in a while.") But opinion divided on whether women should speak in public, even though Finney's revival techniques had helped open up this possibility. Mahan supported the women (especially as his own daughter neared the time of her "commencement essay") but was not able to carry the rest of the faculty. Antoinette Brown, the first woman to be ordained, was only permitted to attend theological lectures "unofficially." But she did attend and completed a theological education. The education Oberlin provided for women laid the foundation for their progressing even further into the women's rights movement. As a result Oberlin graduated many feminists of the era. Among these were Lucy Stone (whose name became notorious as the household expression for a woman who kept her family name in marriage) and Betsy Cowles (president of the Second National Women's Rights Convention).

An interesting sidelight in this story is Oberlin's commitment to "physiological reform." The institution was deeply influenced by the philosophy of the manual labor schools that Theodore Weld had worked to propagate. Students usually had four hours of manual labor daily— to support themselves, to preserve appreciation for physical labor, but primarily for the sake of health. Oberlin was deeply permeated by the health food movement of that time. Shipherd, Stewart, Mahan, Weld, and Finney were all disciples of Sylvester Graham, inventor of the "Graham Cracker." Graham taught total abstinence not only from alcoholic beverages but also from "tobacco, tea, coffee, and all other stimulants," as well as "pepper, mustard, oil, vinegar, etc." Oberlinites tended to be vegetarian, and almost all sweets were outlawed.

Oberlin was also in the vanguard of educational reform. Shipherd had consulted educational reformers in developing plans for the new school. Oberlin prepared teachers for the new "common schools" for the masses. (Horace Mann had effected the founding of the first state-supported "normal school" only in 1839.) In the 1840s innovative new courses in teaching methods were developed. This was not taught in the more traditional schools. Oberlinites advocated a form of "progressive education" that governed by "moral principles, instead of the rod and the rule." Some have credited Oberlin with introducing the study of music to American education. Finney himself was quite musical (he sang, directed choirs, and played the bass viol) and refused to teach at Oberlin unless the first faculty included a professor of music. Oberlin also pioneered in business and agricultural education.

Oberlin was politically committed to the progressive movements of the period. Early members of Oberlin Colony had been conservative Whigs, but antislavery sentiments pushed them in another direction— toward the Liberty Party, an abolitionist third party, and later into the new, antislavery Republican Party. In 1856, the *Oberlin Evangelist* called for support for "Free Press, Free Speech, Free Men, Frémont [an antislavery presidential candidate] and Victory." In most elections the Oberlin Colony voted solidly Republican. This political persuasion put them at odds with the surrounding Democratic political establishment and gave a political cast to Oberlin's commitment to reform.

But the really explosive issue that rocked Oberlin and for which she gained particular notoriety was the civil disobedience she advocated. The doctrine developed gradually as Oberlin supported the Underground Railroad, by which slaves were smuggled through the North to freedom in Canada. This activity climaxed in a court case that played a major role in the development of American civil liberties. But that story deserves separate attention.

5

Civil Disobedience and the Oberlin-Wellington Rescue Case

It is difficult to overstate the extent to which Oberlin identified with the black and the slave—or the extent to which this fact generated opposition to Oberlin's course. When it was announced that students would be admitted irrespective of sex or color, Oberlin's financial agent in New England wrote back that his area would scarcely accept coeducation and that everything possible must be done to avoid the accusation of "amalgamation of the races." He feared that "as soon as your *darkies* begin to come in . . . the whites will begin to leave—and at length your Institute will change colour." Unless this policy were dropped, he warned, the school would "be blown *sky high* and you will have a black establishment there *thro' out*."

Humorist Artemas Ward amused his readers in 1865 by writing that Oberlin was "a very good college" though it was his "onbiassed 'pinion that they go it rather too strong on Ethiopians." His description of the streets in Oberlin had wide circulation. "As a faithful historian, I must menshum the fack that on rainy dase white people can't find their way threw the streets without the gas is lit, ther bein such a numerosity of cullerd pussons in the town."

There was apparently no bar at Oberlin to social intercourse between the races. Black students boarded and roomed with whites. The Ladies' Principal reported in 1866 that the black women "have been seated at different tables by the side of white ladies, and if it so happened opposite white young men." In the 1840s one young male student wrote home that "about every fifth one at the table is a darky" and added that "the best appearing chap I have seen here is black." Artemas Ward no doubt exaggerated in saying that "at the Boarding House the cullard people sit at the first table. What they leave is maid into hash for the white people." But all of this appeared so shocking to the outside that one student had to write home that "we don't have to kiss the Niggars nor speak to them without we are to mind to." But it should be added that while there seem to have been no cases of interracial marriage, there was no special bar to social intercourse of the opposite sexes—and even some reports of romances.

Oberlin, however, struggled with how far to go in identification with the black race, particularly when their concerns pushed them to the edge of legality. The underground railroad especially raised these issues. The college was one of the most important "stations," and hundreds of escaped slaves passed through Oberlin.

The college maintained a Fund for Fugitives, and expenses were often paid out of public funds. Very often faculty homes (even the president's) were used to house escaped slaves. Those who died in Oberlin were buried at public expense in the village cemetery. The town prided itself on never having lost a single "passenger." This was not an easy record to maintain. As early as 1841 Oberlinites were forced to recapture escaped slaves seized by authorities.

All of this ran directly counter to the federal fugitive slave laws that required the return of escaped slaves. Such laws had been on the books since 1793, but the 1830s and '40s saw efforts to tighten up such laws on both the national and the state level. Oberlin's response to this was based on a doctrine of civil disobedience that appealed to "higher" or "divine law." Evangelist Finney himself made major contributions to the development of this doctrine. Historian Charles Cole has called this "one of his chief contributions to the cause" of abolitionism.[1]

In 1839 the Ohio legislature overwhelmingly adopted a statute that in effect extended over all of Ohio the jurisdiction of Kentucky with regard to fugitive slaves. One Oberlin professor had to go into hiding after helping one old black woman to escape. Finney himself introduced a resolution into the next meeting of the Ohio Anti-Slavery Society declaring that such a statute was not "obligatory upon the citizens of this State, inasmuch as its requisitions are a palpable violation of the Constitution of this State, and of the United States, of the common law and of the law of God." The rationale for this affirmation of civil disobedience was spelled out:

Resolved, That for the following obvious reasons, we regard it, as a well settled principle of both common and constitutional law, that no human legislation can annul, or set aside the law or authority of God.

   a. The most able writers on elementary law, have laid it down as a first principle, that whatever is contrary to the law of God, is not law.

   b. Where a bond, or other written instrument, or anything else, is of immoral tendency, courts of law have refused to recognize it as legal and obligatory.

   c. The administration of oaths, or affirmations, in courts of justice, is a recognition of the existence and supreme authority of God.

   d. The Constitution of this State expressly recognizes the axiom, that no human enactment can bend the conscience, or set aside our obligations to God.

   e. The general instrument of which the federal Government is founded, recognizes the same truth—that rights conferred by our Creator as inalienable, can never be cancelled, or set aside by human enactments.

   f. The administration of oaths, or affirmations in all departments of the general and state government, is a recognition of the truth, that God's authority is supreme.

1. Charles C. Cole Jr., *The Social Ideas of the Northern Evangelists 1826–1860* (New York: Columbia University Press, 1954), 208.

Finney's convictions, if anything, grew stronger over the years. Oberlin was particularly offended by the federal Fugitive Slave Law of 1850. Finney called it the "Fugitive Slave Bill" even after it was passed, arguing that nothing so opposed to the divine will and the United States Constitution should ever be called a law. He wrote such convictions into his *Lectures on Systematic Theology*, insisting that "no human constitution or enactment can, by any possibility, be law that recognizes the right of one human being to enslave another." Finney argued, "We are bound in all cases to disobey, when human legislation contravenes moral law, or invades the rights of conscience."

The whole campus was embroiled in these issues. During the 1850s the literary societies debated such propositions as "Ought Christians to obey the new Fugitive Law?"; "Ought a functionary of the government either to execute a law which in his opinion conflicts with the divine law or else resign his office?"; "Ought we to resist by violence the execution of the Fugitive Slave Law?"; and "Does the injustice of a law free the citizens of the US from the moral obligation to obey it?"

Students (and faculty) engaged in civil disobedience, not only in the Underground Railroad and by recapturing escaped slaves seized by the authorities but also in some cases by invading the South to free slaves. George Thompson served five years in a Missouri penitentiary for trying to help two slaves escape to Illinois. Calvin Fairbank claimed to have liberated forty-seven slaves but served two prison terms of four and twelve years for such activities. The climax of these efforts was the notorious "Oberlin-Wellington Rescue Case," which gained for Oberlin a worldwide reputation.

In early 1858 John Price, a fugitive slave, sought refuge in Oberlin. That summer four armed men from the South paid a teenager to lure Price out of town, ostensibly to help dig up some potatoes. Once outside of Oberlin, Price was seized and taken to nearby Wellington to await the next train. Fortunately Oberlinites returning to town met the fleeing party on its way to Wellington and divined what had happened. By ringing the chapel bell, they alerted the colony, and a crowd of several hundred gathered in Wellington. The situation presented a conflict of values for the largely nonviolent Oberlinites, but after some hesitation the hotel was stormed, and Price was rescued without, in the words of one narrator, "so much as bruising a finger." Price was rushed back to Oberlin and hidden in the home of J. H. Fairchild (professor of moral and mental philosophy and Finney's successor as president) before being spirited off to Canada.

Such a flagrant challenge to federal authority could not remain unpunished. For the local Democratic establishment, it provided a chance to "get" Republican Oberlin, to strike a major blow at the Underground Railroad, and to demonstrate a willingness to enforce the unpopular fugitive slave laws. Indictments were brought against twenty-one identifiable citizens of Oberlin as well as against some residents of Wellington (though these were not pressed so that the trial could focus exclusively on Oberlin and play on the local resentment of Oberlinism). Among the Oberlinites indicted were Henry E. Peck, associate professor of mental and moral philosophy (Oberlin's professor of Christian ethics), and James M. Fitch, Oberlin's Sunday school superintendent. The trial opened on April 5, 1859, and quickly degenerated into a political struggle (jury, judge, and prosecutors were all Democrats ideologically opposed to Oberlin) and a propaganda battle whose volleys were heard around the world.

The district attorney portrayed the Oberlinites as revolutionaries, characterized the "higher law" as the "Devil's law," and claimed that "Higher Law people ran into the predicament of free love and infidelity." He advised the Oberlinites to preach "the Bible and not politics." Replying to accusations that their actions were unpatriotic, Peck denied that "there is no patriotism where there is not an acknowledgment of the maxim, 'Our country right or wrong,'" and insisted that he was a follower of a "higher patriotism" that sought to keep the country honest and true to its highest ideals and revolutionary convictions. The Oberlin defense explicitly advocated the doctrine of a divine or "higher law" but rested most of its case on such issues as the questionable identification of Price and the constitutionality of the Fugitive Slave Law.

But unavoidably some of the argument focused on the question of the "higher law." Peck insisted, "We must obey God always, and human law, social and civil, when we can." This "Divine Will was well expounded in the life of Christ," whose gospel was such that "those who should follow Him, should minister to the needy; that the poor and forlorn would be blessed by it; that those 'sick and in prison' would be cheered by it; and that it would strike the iron from countless wretches unjustly bound."

The Oberlin prisoners did manage several astute propaganda coups. (Their imprisonment was in part because, to dramatize the fact they were in jail for their convictions, they refused to post bail.) Urgent appeals to the state and federal courts were unsuccessful but did publicize the case. Money poured into the defense fund from around the world. The prisoners used their confinement to create the aura of martyrdom. They published a paper from their jail in Cleveland. (Fortunately their jailer was antislavery in conviction and sympathetic to their cause!) This paper, titled *The Rescuer,* expounded "the nature and claims of the

Cleveland Jail: site where Oberlin rescuers were incarcerated for disobeying the Fugitive Slave Law

Higher Law, the iniquities of American slavery, and the injustice and illegality of the Fugitive Slave Act." But perhaps the greatest coup on behalf of the prisoners was bringing four hundred "Sabbath school children" to march through the streets of Cleveland with banners before visiting the jail to have services with their imprisoned Sunday school superintendent James M. Fitch. Ethics professor Peck was allowed to preach to crowds gathered in the jail yard.

But political power still reigned, and it looked as if the Oberlinites would be convicted until someone came up with the ploy of arresting the four "slave-catchers" and bringing them to trial in Oberlin for kidnapping. In Oberlin the judge, jury, and prosecutors would all be Republican, operating on a different interpretation of the constitutionality of the Fugitive Slave Law. Conviction was certain, and the trial would prevent the major witnesses in the government's case from appearing in the Cleveland court. Just to be sure that their prisoners were not released before the trial, the sheriff on whom the papers would have to be served left town for several days. The situation was finally resolved by dropping both sets of charges and releasing both sets of prisoners. The Oberlinites returned triumphantly to Oberlin to celebrate their victory while the *Cleveland Plain Dealer* bitterly complained that "the government has been beaten at last with law, Justice, and facts all on its side, and Oberlin, with its rebellious high law creed, is triumphant."

The Oberlin-Wellington Rescue Case, however, proved to be a major force for raising consciousness on the issue of slavery. One historian of Oberlin has ranked the episode with the publication of *Uncle Tom's Cabin* and John Brown's raid on Harper's Ferry as events that stirred the public imagination before the Civil War. William Lloyd Garrison wrote his greetings in these words: "What a humiliating spectacle is presented to the world in the trials now going on at Cleveland of your humane and Christian citizens who so nobly delivered the spoiled out of the hands of the oppressor! . . . But this very persecution will give a fresh impetus to our noble cause." And so it did. But the importance of the Oberlin-Wellington Rescue Case is not confined to its impact in that period on the awareness of the slavery problem. A record of the case was reprinted in the 1970s as a landmark in the development of American civil liberties.

The experiences of the Oberlinites in this case pushed them even closer to a position that can only be called revolutionary. During the trial the Oberlin students began to debate such questions as "Resolved that it is the duty of the citizens of Oberlin to forcibly resist the Fugitive Slave Law, henceforth and forever." They also began to consider whether the Oberlin prisoners should be released by force. One defense lawyer argued for "the right of revolution, the ultimate and legitimate resort of people who find their governments too oppressive longer to be borne." In this the Oberlinites appealed to the precedent of American revolutionary origins. As one of the prisoners put it:

> We belong to no "modern school" of politics or theology, and lay claim
> to no new light on these subjects. We belong to the school of the Fathers,
> who having been driven from their native land by the persecutions of

their government, taught their children that "resistance to tyrants is obedience to God"; or to the more ancient school, which exclaimed to the existing authorities, "Whether it be right to hearken unto you more than unto God, judge ye"; or to that still more ancient, which said to the king, "We will not serve thy Gods nor worship the golden image which thou hast set up."

Such teachings enabled Oberlin to sympathize with John Brown, who had been preparing for his raid on Harper's Ferry during the Oberlin-Wellington Rescue Trial. Two Oberlin blacks, harness maker Lewis Sheridan Leary and student John A. Copeland, died in that episode. Leary was killed during the raid, and Copeland was executed a few days later. The chapel bell tolled for an hour on the day of Brown's execution. The student paper reported that in a memorial service "Professor Peck surpassed himself. . . . His summer's incarceration has given him a rich experience from which to draw, when about to speak for the downtrodden, or account the deeds of the martyrs of liberty." A member of the board of trustees declared in a funeral sermon that "we can see no signs of hallucination or of infatuation in John Brown. We esteem him as one of the Wise Men of our times." At a joint meeting of the men's literary societies, one toast to John Brown was in these words: "to John Brown: the hero of Harper's Ferry—the true representative of the American idea!"

Postscript by Douglas M. Strong

The Oberlin-Wellington case represented just a fraction of civil disobedience incidents initiated by evangelicals and others in the antebellum era, especially after the passage of the Fugitive Slave Law, the most controversial act to result from Congress's infamous Compromise of 1850. Attempts by slaves to escape from bondage—both successfully and unsuccessfully—received supportive assistance from free blacks and whites for decades. Most Northerners turned a blind eye to these ostensibly illegal actions. But after the enactment of the much more stringent 1850 federal statute, the legal efforts to re-enslave fugitives by law enforcement became more coordinated. In opposition, rescue efforts also became more overt, and the stage was set for increasing numbers of abolitionists willing to go against the federal law in order to obey a "higher law."

Though never constituted as an official organization, the underground railroad nonetheless flourished as an informal network of women and men who assisted bondsmen to freedom. Most of these sympathizing disobeyers of the Fugitive Slave Law were Quakers or abolitionist evangelicals—Methodists (especially those from the African Methodist Episcopal, African Methodist Episcopal Zion, and Wesleyan Methodist churches), Baptists (especially Freewill Baptists), Congregationalists, and Presbyterians. Among the many African American underground railroad "conductors" who demonstrated evangelical piety were Henry Bibb, Henry "Box" Brown, Josiah Henson, Jermain Loguen, Wil-

Laura Smith Haviland: founder of an interracial school and "conductor" on the Underground Railroad

liam Still, and Harriet Tubman. Some of the white evangelical rescuers, in addition to the Oberlinites mentioned in this chapter, included John G. Fee, Luther Lee, John Rankin, Gerrit Smith, Charles Torrey, and Delia Webster. But two of the most compelling evangelical abolitionists who participated in this type of civil disobedience (that is, the unlawful rescue of fleeing slaves) deserve particular recognition—Laura Smith Haviland and Samuel Ringgold Ward.

Raised in the Society of Friends (Quakers), Laura Smith Haviland had a dramatic conversion to evangelical Christianity as an adolescent; later, she joined the Wesleyan Methodists. The Wesleyans represented an ideal denominational home for Haviland, since they expressed both the social reform commitments she admired from her Quaker background and the revivalistic affective piety she came to see as central to her evangelical relationship with God. Laura Haviland and her husband, Charles, established Raisin Institute, the first interracial school in Michigan. They also held the distinction of being the first conductors of runaway slaves in Michigan, eventually sending fugitives on their way to Canada when the 1850 law made it impossible for escaped African Americans to remain safely in the United States. After Charles's early death, Laura Haviland continued her rescue work, and even increased it, by traveling to Ohio and elsewhere in order to convey slaves to freedom. Her bold flouting of the Fugitive Slave Law became notorious in the South, so much so that several slave owners placed a price on her head. Haviland was never caught, though, and she lived out her days after the Civil War working with African Americans.

Samuel Ringgold Ward: evangelical abolitionist pastor and reformer

Though similar in some respects to Haviland's activist evangelicalism, Samuel Ringgold Ward's story exhibits significant differences because he was African American. Ward's parents fled slavery when he was only a toddler, making him technically a fugitive; the foreboding associated with this dreadful status haunted him throughout his life. Like Haviland, Ward had an adolescent conversion to Christ. Ward received a license to preach as a Congregationalist minister and then, while still in his twenties, he served as the pastor of two all-white churches in central New York State—an extremely unusual occurrence in the 1840s. In South Butler, where one of his churches was located,

Ward and his family were the only African Americans in the entire town. As a staunch evangelical, Ward regularly preached revivalistic sermons for conversion, with the result that the South Butler congregation tripled its membership during his pastorate. Meanwhile, as a social reformer, Ward led his members to embrace abolitionism, to support the Liberty Party, and to offer their church as an active "station" on the Underground Railroad. A few years later, in 1851, when Ward lived in Syracuse, he assisted his white friend Gerrit Smith and other abolitionist citizens in a highly publicized scheme to release a runaway held in the city jail and then hustle the slave off to Canada. Ward's participation in this plot exposed his own lifelong fugitive status, forcing him to flee to Canada, too. He never returned to the United States. Though a few white abolitionists were imprisoned for conducting fugitive slaves, the dangerous ramifications of disobeying the law of the land fell much more harshly on African Americans.

Religiously motivated civil disobedience became prominent again during the civil rights struggle of the 1950s and '60s. Freedom Rides to the South symbolized the reverse journey of those who had ridden north for freedom a century earlier. Like their predecessors, these antisegregationist social reformers faced the consequences of disregarding and violating the law for the sake of their conscience, as it will for anyone whose faith compels them to go against the legal norms of the society.

6

Arthur and Lewis Tappan

The Businessman as Reformer

Contemporary stereotypes are shaken by the realization that the major financial backing and organizational leadership behind the abolitionist crusade derived from the man who founded Dun & Bradstreet (the Wall Street credit rating firm) and his silk-merchant brother. Lewis and Arthur Tappan were two of the most prominent and wealthy businessmen in pre–Civil War New York. Yet these two men so threw themselves into the reform movements of the era that one tribute after Arthur's death affirmed that "in the slavery agitation, its beginning, its extent, its power, its results, it may be said, without a question, that Arthur Tappan was the pivotal centre of the whole movement."

The Tappan brothers were born in the late 1780s into a large and pious family in Northampton, Massachusetts. The Tappans lived there for a time in the old house of Jonathan Edwards—not inappropriately—in view of the deep Edwardian piety that permeated the home under the influence of their mother, Sarah Tappan. Later, as apprenticed clerks in Boston, the brothers sat for a while under the preaching of Unitarian William Ellery Channing. Lewis at first embraced Unitarianism, serving in 1825 as treasurer of the American Unitarian Association. But in 1828 he returned to evangelicalism, explaining his action publicly in a *Letter from a Gentleman in Boston to a Unitarian Clergyman of That City.*

In New York the Tappan brothers later became the major financial supporters of evangelist Charles G. Finney, funding many of his pet projects. Lewis and Arthur Tappan were consistent advocates and practitioners of a form of evangelical religion that, like the Evangelical Revival of the preceding century, found a positive role theologically for "good works." Lewis described the faith of his brother: "With a firm belief in the evangelical faith, he relied upon the mercy of God through the atoning sacrifice of the Saviour, discarding all thoughts of his good deeds as meriting reward in another life, although he firmly believed that as evidences of piety they were essential."

It is difficult to overestimate the impact of the Tappans upon both the business community and the reform movements. Their fortunes were made in Arthur's silk company (the largest silk jobber in the country), where their success was a result of absolute honesty, a preference for "cash sales," and a new system of "fixed prices." The Tappans pioneered in fixed prices for all customers instead of haggling and deals. Customers knew what to expect, and strangers could trust them. By the high-volume and low-markup formula of a modern K-Mart, the Tappans grew rich, grossing more than a million dollars a year.

Their business survived a devastating fire only to go under in the financial collapse of 1837. Arthur Tappan suspended payments owing more than a million dollars, but within eighteen months he was back on his feet, having paid all his obligations with interest. Arthur was also the founder of the *Journal of Commerce* in 1827, a new daily to "exert a wholesome moral influence" by "abstaining particularly from publishing immoral advertisements" for such things as "spiritous liquors, circuses, and theatres."

Lewis Tappan set out on his own in 1841 by founding the Mercantile Agency (the antecedent of today's Dun & Bradstreet). This company set up a network of contacts throughout the country to provide credit ratings for businessmen. In an increasingly mobile and widespread economy, this new idea helped provide stability when personal knowledge of businessmen was no longer available by enquiry around the local community.

In spite of such wealth the Tappan brothers preferred to live unostentatiously, considering themselves stewards of the money God had given them. Lewis Tappan authored late in his life a pamphlet titled *Is It Right to Be Rich?* (1869), answering the question largely in the negative in an effort to combat a less "responsible" postwar pattern of the accumulation of wealth. All of their lives the Tappans plowed most of their wealth back into various philanthropies, benevolent societies, and social reform movements.

Arthur Tappan especially made major contributions to these groups and served many as officer or board member. With an anonymous gift to the American Bible Society he hoped "to supply every family in the United States with a Bible." He supported the American Sunday School Union, encouraging it to "have a Sabbath School formed within two years in every town" in the newly settled Mississippi Valley. His contributions to the American Tract Society went for presses and printing of materials—he wanted to "give two tracts to every family in the valley of the Mississippi." Tappan also attempted to fight prostitution and rescue its practitioners by founding a Magdalen Society modeled after a British counterpart. But an 1831 report of the society was so explicit and devastating that public reaction forced him to back off from this project.

The Tappan brothers were a little severe and humorless, given to a scrupulosity that sometimes annoyed their colleagues—even those also devoted to the same benevolent enterprises. They were committed to the Temperance Movement, and Arthur led the campaign to replace communion wine with a "nonalcoholic burgundy" that he had especially imported from France—a cause much mocked in the New York press. He was also active in the General Union for Promoting the Observance of the Christian Sabbath. In this work he opposed laws requiring postal clerks to work on Sunday, supported the founding of a new six-day stage line so that Christians would not have to patronize those that operated on Sunday, advocated boycotting products made on Sunday, and so on. But what really annoyed some ministers was his questioning whether churches should allow themselves the luxury of being lit with gas from companies using Sunday labor. Arthur was not at all amused when a churchman questioned whether silk goods were immoral since they were luxury items produced by silkworms that worked on Sunday.

But more significant was Tappan support for the "free church" movement in New York City. This little-known aspect of American church history was a protest against selling and renting pews to support the construction and maintenance of church buildings. (For more on this movement, see chap. 9.) Opponents of this practice argued that the result was the exclusion (or at least embarrassment) of the poor and a seating pattern according to wealth that could not be squared with biblical teachings against "being a respector of persons" or giving preference to wealth and status. Such sentiments led a number of Presbyterian ministers to found in 1830 in New York City a "Third Presbytery" consisting of "free churches" where pews were open to all regardless of class or wealth. Within two years these missions boasted a membership of nearly four thousand.

The Tappan brothers put up much of the money for these churches. The second of six such churches founded was a remodeled theater called the Chatham Street Chapel. This church had been prepared especially for evangelist Charles G. Finney when the Tappans finally convinced him to take a settled pastorate in New York City after his revivals in the West and upstate New York. The pastors of the "free churches" were all practitioners of Finney's "new measure" revivalism, and the congregations consisted largely of converts from Finney's campaigns. These churches were closely identified with the reform movements, providing finances, hosting abolitionist conventions and other rallies, and producing the troops of the movements.

The extent of Lewis Tappan's commitment to the egalitarianism implicit in the "free church" movement can be judged from one of his disagreements with the church. Lewis Tappan wrote in one letter that "some of us thought that the 'negro Pew' should be done away—for although people were invited to sit where they pleased, it was understood, by whites and blacks, that the colored people should sit by themselves in a certain place in the galleries. . . . In the Chatham St. Chapel we succeeded in bringing the colored part of the congregation downstairs to occupy a range of slips on one side of the church, but were never able, though Mr. Finney was the pastor, to abolish the distinction altogether, in seats, and allow the people to sit, in fact, as they were invited to, wherever they chose. . . . Finding nothing could be done in a matter so near to my heart I left the church."

Such concerns found a major outlet in the abolitionist struggles. This reform increasingly absorbed the time and wealth of the Tappan brothers. They had long been concerned about the slavery issue in a general way. They supported for a time the American Colonization Society—though in part it must be admitted because of their interest in opening up new areas of trade among the freed slaves attempting to establish Liberia. But the Tappans gradually withdrew from this movement. Arthur disapproved of the rum trade that had become an essential part of the Liberian economy, but Lewis felt that such a program was basically an escape from the deeper issues of race and equality. When the school of immediate abolitionism arose, the Tappans soon transferred their allegiance (and financial support!) to this more radical approach.

When William Lloyd Garrison was imprisoned for libel, Arthur Tappan bailed him out. The resulting contact with Garrison and his thought drew Tappan toward immediate abolitionism and generated a small contribution toward the founding of the *Liberator*. Lewis was drawn into the movement by Theodore Weld. Finney had suggested that Lewis Tappan send his sons to the Oneida Institute in western New York. Oneida was operated by Finney's theological mentor, George Washington Gale, and the Tappan boys were converted there under the influence of Weld. When Lewis Tappan came up for commencement exercises, he met Weld, and the two men soon became close friends and coworkers in the antislavery struggle.

These growing convictions climaxed in the 1833 founding of the New York Anti-Slavery Society by the Tappans, Garrison, and a number of other revival and reform leaders. Though Arthur had been a major contributor to its construction, the trustees of Clinton Hall

objected to his leasing the building for an abolitionist meeting, forcing a last-minute move to Finney's Chatham Street Chapel. While
an anti-abolitionist mob mistakenly gathered outside Clinton Hall,
the abolitionists in the church quickly adopted a constitution and
elected Arthur Tappan president before dispersing into the night. A
few abolitionists who had retired to an upstairs Sunday school room
had to be rescued by the police when the mob discovered they had
been misled and descended on the church.

By the end of the year, sufficient interest had been generated to
found a national society. Sixty delegates gathered in Philadelphia to
promulgate a "Declaration of Sentiments" authored by Garrison that
included the pledge to do "all that in us lies, consistently with this
Declaration of our principles, to overthrow the most execrable system
of slavery that has ever been witnessed upon earth . . . and to secure
to the colored population of the United States, all the rights and privileges which belong to them as men, and as Americans—come what
may to our persons, our interest, or our reputations." Arthur Tappan was also elected president of this new society, and the American
Anti-Slavery Society had come into being.

Meanwhile the Tappans had been supporting Theodore Weld and a
new seminary in Cincinnati that they hoped would become a citadel in
the West of their revivalist and reform ideals. But when Lane Seminary
trustees forbade the discussion of slavery, and Weld and his supporters withdrew rather than submit, Arthur Tappan shifted his support
to the Lane Rebels and reneged on his commitment to the seminary.
When Oberlin College emerged as a refuge for the radical students,
Tappan convinced Finney to accept the professorship of theology, a
chair that he offered to underwrite financially. Tappan also laid down
the condition that Oberlin remain committed to "the broad ground
of moral reform, in all its departments" and admit black students on
an equal basis with whites.

Oberlin was very important to Tappan. He pledged his entire
income (about one hundred thousand dollars a year—quite a sum
in those days!) to the project, holding back only enough to provide
modestly for his family. Unfortunately the business collapse of 1837
prevented Arthur from fulfilling his pledge. But by that time the school

had been launched, and as Finney later put it, "Although Arthur Tappan failed to do for Oberlin all that he intended, yet his *promise* was the condition of the existence of Oberlin *as it has been*," the major center of antislavery activity in the West and a crucial force in the abolitionizing of the North.

Tappan money and organizational skill were also behind the abolitionist propaganda campaigns. Lewis Tappan created the plan of publishing four monthly journals (one to be issued each week) to be mailed free to influential persons throughout the country. This more than any other abolitionist activity united the South in opposition. Mobs broke into post offices to destroy shipments of the journals.

The Tappans had already come to expect such resistance. A mob had earlier ransacked Lewis's home, burning his furniture in the streets. (Mrs. Tappan found a bright spot in the event: the mob had destroyed some expensive-looking items that Lewis had always felt were too ostentatious for the frequent prayer meetings held in the home.) Tappan left his home unrepaired all summer as a "silent Anti-Slavery preacher to the crowds who will flock to see it." But this was nothing compared to the opposition to the postal campaign.

Southern officials insisted on the extradition of Arthur Tappan to face charges of fomenting a slave rebellion. One Southern minister offered one hundred thousand dollars for the deliverance to New Orleans of Arthur Tappan and abolitionist editor La Roy Sunderland (later a founder of the abolitionist Wesleyan Methodist Connection; see chap. 7). Tappan responded to this offer with a rare burst of humor: "If that sum is placed in a New York bank, I may possibly think of giving myself up." The Tappans lived in fear of assassination or destruction of their property. They had to seek insurance out of the city in Boston at an "abolitionist premium." When the South began to boycott the Tappans' business enterprises and threatened the broadening of economic sanctions to those with whom they did business, the New York business community panicked and sent delegates to plead with the Tappans to give up their antislavery labors. To one party of this steady procession of visitors Arthur Tappan was heard to reply, "You demand that I shall cease my anti-slavery labors. . . . I *will be hung first*." Opposition seemed only to steel the

Tappan brothers in their convictions, propelling them into ever more controversial involvements.

Lewis Tappan, for example, became a major figure in the Amistad Case. The *Amistad* (Spanish for "friendship") was a ship that had been built especially for the slave trade. While being transported from Havana to Guanaja (in eastern Cuba), nearly fifty slaves had mutinied, killing the captain and the cook and imprisoning the Cuban crew. Under the leadership of Joseph Cinqué (apparently the source of the name adopted by "General Field Marshall Cinque" of the Patty Hearst kidnappers), the Africans tried to sail for Africa while the Cubans tried to alter the course toward a sympathetic state in the South. The ship ended up near Long Island, where the United States Navy seized it.

Lewis Tappan: Christian businessman and entrepreneur who financed and led many social causes

This incident gripped the attention not only of the American public, but also of the whole Western world. American prejudices against Africans were strong (were they not murderers and perhaps even cannibals?), and major questions about the future of the slave trade would depend on how the United States government handled the case. Lewis Tappan immediately formed a committee for the defense of the blacks and took upon himself their physical and spiritual care. He carried the case all the way to the Supreme Court and then raised money to send the blacks back to their homes in Africa—along with a few missionaries from Oberlin.

The Amistad Case led directly into another philanthropy of Lewis Tappan. The Tappan brothers had become increasingly disenchanted with the benevolent societies. The American Bible Society had refused to make slaves and freedmen particular objects of Scripture distribution. The American Tract Society had not only refused to issue abolitionist tracts, but had also edited out offending passages in British materials. The missionary societies did not hesitate to send out proslavery missionaries. After failing in his efforts to change such practices, Lewis Tappan finally moved toward founding a separate antislavery missionary society. The Amistad committee was merged into a few other organizations to form the American Missionary Association (AMA), a "living protest" against the societies that refused to take a stand on slavery.

Lewis Tappan said of the AMA that "its single object is to send out a pure gospel free from any compromise." The AMA supported as many as two hundred missionaries (including a number sent to the South) and expended a million dollars in its first decade. Though not always able to break completely out of the paternalistic mold, this society was far in advance of its time. Tappan asked abolitionist Amos Phelps for advice in running the West Indian mission. Among the principles advocated in Phelps's report was "dealing with the people in all things as men and not as serviles." This included enabling them to find economic self-sufficiency and encouraging the missionaries to avoid expensive, comfortable quarters, in order to "identify themselves with the people."

The American Missionary Association attempted to express the goals of equality to which the Tappans had long been committed (often in advance of other abolitionists who wished to rid the country of the sin of slavery, but had no interest in "social intercourse"). For the Tappans the abolitionist struggle was not just against slavery but also explicitly against "prejudice" and the "hateful caste feeling that so extensively prevailed in the country." Lewis Tappan was especially concerned that children be raised sensitive to the issue of race so that as adults they would "be able to meet at the polls, sit on juries, attend political meetings, practice at the bar, unite in processions, and mingle with their fellow-men in the various walks of life, on equal terms, as the religion of Jesus, and the laws of the land require."

These sentiments were touchingly expressed by Lewis Tappan at age seventy-five during an Emancipation Jubilee in 1863. After reviewing with some nostalgia the antislavery struggle, Lewis commented that some claimed that blacks were superior to whites in intelligence and strength, but Tappan wasn't so sure and believed that "a white man was just as good as a black man, if he behaved himself." After the cheers and laughter subsided, Tappan closed with a verse of poetry:

> Judge not of virtue by the name,
> Or think to read it on the skin;
> Honor in white and black the same—
> the stamp of glory is within.

Postscript by Douglas M. Strong

Lewis Tappan's deep conviction that every human being is made in the image of God fueled his hatred of slavery and the racist "caste system" that supported it. This commitment to the full equality of all people animated his philanthropic work. It also motivated him to be a successful businessperson. Tappan was convinced that the profits he made as a publisher and financier allowed him to do good by funding a wide variety of reform movements. And his calculation was correct; his wealth became the financial backbone for the reform activities of Finney, Oberlin College, and many abolitionist organizations. In this way, the Tappan brothers' belief that businesspeople could (and, as Christians, should) be social reformers provides an example for businesses today. Emerging adult Christians are expressing enormous interest in social entrepreneurship and social venture capitalism, which—like the enterprises of the Tappans—seek to find ways to fund justice-oriented projects through both traditional and nontraditional business models.

Lewis Tappan's heartfelt belief in the human dignity of every person also spurred his activism on behalf of the Africans who were captured in 1839 after mutinying on board the slave ship *Amistad* (described above). Steven Spielberg produced an inspiring 1997 historical drama about the incident, but unfortunately, the movie fails to capture accurately the influence of Tappan and other evangelical reformers. First, the film repeatedly shows Christians—who are mostly elderly and (in the words of one of the characters) "miserable looking"—attempting to visit the slaves during their incarceration. The evangelicals are caricatured by droning a doleful version of "Amazing Grace" and literally pushing Bibles at the prisoners. Later in the movie, Tappan is depicted as a patronizing abolitionist who is more interested in pursuing duty than in caring for the plight of the Africans. The character supposedly representing Tappan states: "It is our destiny as abolitionists and as Christians to save these people. . . . Christ went to the cross to make a statement and so must we." Tappan is shown as aloof to the slaves' situation, in contrast to John Quincy Adams. The movie portrays Adams as desiring to discover the humanity of the slaves, while the Tappan character says that the prisoners "may be more valuable to our cause in death than in life"—as martyrs, thereby treating them as pawns in a larger political power play. In actuality, Tappan came to know and care for the Amistad Africans personally and bankrolled their entire law case, as well as many other causes on behalf of slaves. It was Tappan—and not another character, as the film depicts—who spent many days searching the ships and wharves of New York harbor in order to find an interpreter for the Africans, finally locating a young British sailor of West African background who spoke their Mendi language. After the Africans were freed by the Supreme Court in 1841 and were ready to depart, again it was Lewis Tappan who, along with an African American pastor, J. W. C. Pennington, secured the funds for their voyage. As the Mendi people left New York for their home, Tappan and several other evangelical abolitionists who had worked closely with the Africans for two years prayed God's blessing on them and on "thy native land."[1] Tappan's faith compelled him to affirm the full humanity of all people, both personally and with his finances.

---

1. Bertram Wyatt-Brown, *Lewis Tappan and the Evangelical War against Slavery* (Cleveland: Case Western Reserve University Press, 1969), 205–20.

7

Orange Scott, Luther Lee, and the Wesleyan Methodists

In January 1844, the *Oberlin Evangelist* took delight in noticing the appearance of a new paper they had received on exchange as a professional courtesy, the *True Wesleyan*. The *True Wesleyan* spoke for a group that had seceded the previous year from the Methodist Episcopal Church under the leadership of such men as Orange Scott, Jotham Horton, and Luther Lee. Of these men the *Evangelist* commented that "their open and fearless advocacy of the claims of truth, justice and downtrodden humanity, endeared them to the hearts of all true philanthropists" and of the paper that "in it, the claims of the Lord's poor and oppressed ones have their proper place."

Within the somewhat interrelated contexts of Congregationalism and Presbyterianism, Oberlin had led the abolitionist struggle without spinning off to form a new denomination (though it played a part in the New School/Old School split). Within Methodism, however, the antislavery struggle produced a new antislavery denomination, the Wesleyan Methodist Connection of America, surely one of the few churches in Christian history to be founded squarely on a social issue. The Wesleyan Methodists emerged explicitly as a protest against Methodist compromise on the question of slavery.

Early Methodism had been characterized by vigorous opposition to slavery. As early as 1743 Wesley had written into his "General Rules" a prohibition against "buying and selling the bodies and souls of men, women and children, with an intention to enslave them." His 1774 *Thoughts upon Slavery* condemned

> *every gentleman that has an estate in our American plantations; yea,* ALL SLAVEHOLDERS OF WHATEVER RANK AND DEGREE; *seeing men-buyers are exactly on a level with man-stealers. You therefore are guilty, yea* PRINCIPALLY GUILTY, *of all these frauds, robberies, and murders.* You are the spring that puts all the rest into motion.

Wesley's last letter, written just a few days before his death, encouraged William Wilberforce in his fight against "that execrable villainy" in these words: "Go on, in the name of God, and in the power of his might, till even American slavery (the vilest that ever saw the sun) shall vanish away before it."

American Methodism attempted at first to maintain these convictions. The 1784 founding conference of the Methodist Episcopal Church had called for the expulsion of any member engaging in the slave trade, but with the growth of Methodism into the largest American denomination, this stance was gradually abandoned. When faced with the alternative of growth into a national church or maintaining discipline on the slavery issue, Methodism chose growth and prosperity. By the 1820s and 1830s the Methodists had largely accommodated to the institution of slavery, maintaining at most a nominal disapproval preserved in the *Discipline.*

But the growth of abolitionism in the 1830s again sensitized the consciences of some Methodists. Foremost among these was Orange Scott. Born into a penniless Vermont home in 1800, Scott had received only a few scattered months of education and was not converted until the age of twenty-one. But he gave himself immediately to the Methodist ministry and, despite handicaps in background and education, developed into a powerful leader and preacher. By 1830 he was elected presiding elder (a sort of "district superintendent"), and some were beginning to predict that he would one day be a bishop.

But this promising church career was interrupted by a "crisis of conscience." At the age of thirty-three, Orange Scott became an abolitionist. Though "ashamed to confess it" later, Scott lamented that until that time he had been "ignorant of some important principles or features of civil rights." As he expressed himself years afterward on his deathbed, "being wholly devoted to the one idea of saving souls, I omitted to examine, faithfully and critically as I should, the condition of the country in respect to great moral evils. My eyes, however, were at length opened."

Scott studied the *Liberator* of William Lloyd Garrison and other abolitionist writings for a year before declaring himself an abolitionist. He then spent one hundred dollars of his own money (no small amount in that time for a Methodist preacher!) to subscribe to the *Liberator* for three months in the name of one hundred ministers of the New England Conference. Before the subscriptions expired, a majority of the conference had been "radicalized." As a result the New England delegation to the General Conference of 1836 was abolitionist and included Orange Scott.

Here real confrontation began, and Scott was propelled into national leadership as the key figure in extended debates on slavery. Though one observer characterized his debating as "a noble and lofty effort; calm, dignified, generous, Christian," his opponents insisted that Scott was either a "reckless incendiary or *non compos mentis* ['not of sound mind']." One opponent was heard to mutter somewhat euphemistically on the conference floor, "I wish *to God* he were in heaven." But in spite of Scott's efforts, the conference delegates resolved (by a vote of 120 to 14) to express themselves as "decidedly opposed to modern abolitionism, and wholly disclaim any right, wish or intention to interfere in the Civil and political relationship between master and slave, as it exists in the slave-holding States of the Union." The intent of this motion was made clear when the conference refused an amendment proposed by Scott and others that would add words taken directly from the *Discipline* to the effect that "we are as much as ever convinced of the great evil of slavery."

This resolution became the excuse for the suppression of antislavery discussion within the Methodist Episcopal Church. That year Scott's bishop said that he would reappoint Scott to the presiding eldership only if he would cease lecturing and writing on the subject of slavery. Scott refused and was demoted. Elsewhere bishops and church leaders refused to allow antislavery resolutions to come to the floor of annual conferences, assigned abolitionist ministers either to "hardscrabble" circuits or to churches where the anti-abolitionist feeling was so strong that they would be crushed, brought ministers to trial for attending abolitionist meetings or even reading abolitionist literature, and so on.

Feelings were intense during this period. Those opposing the abolitionists viewed them with real fear. One attack was titled *Abolition a Sedition* and protested the argument that "slavery is wrong by a higher and more imperative law than that of the country," insisting that such a position led to an unconstitutional intrusion of religion into the civil realm. Abolitionism, moreover, distorted the true nature of Christianity, for "it is to the *conservative* power of Christianity that we owe our greatest blessings." The author feared, too, that the abolitionist movement possessed the seeds of anarchy, because it advocated the leveling of "all distinctions in society, of rank, color, caste, and *sex*."

The tensions mounted. The abolitionists insisted that slavery was "sin" and that the churches were the "bulwark of slavery." Their opponents feared anarchy and saw the abolitionists as "subversives" destroying all semblance of "law and order." The pressures on the abolitionists became unbearable, and Scott himself left the ministry for two years to serve as one of the Seventy agents sent out by the American Anti-Slavery Society to spread the gospel of abolitionism. But Scott insisted that though "I closed up and left the 'regular work' of a stationed preacher . . . I still profess to be engaged in the 'regular and appropriate work' of a *gospel minister*."

Scott returned to his church in 1839, but by this time sentiment was growing for the establishment of a new Methodist body that was "truly Wesleyan" and unflinchingly devoted to reform principles. At first these ministers tried to avoid the charge of schism, arguing that it was more to the point to insist that "anti-abolitionist measures tend to schism." But after a long struggle Scott finally decided that there was no alternative but to "stand forth for a new anti-slavery, anti-intemperance, anti-everything-wrong church organization," and the Wesleyan Methodist Connection was formed in the early 1840s.

It is difficult now to re-create the ethos and style of this new denomination. Though focused on the issue of slavery, they became "universal reformers." Their spirit can be seen in the title of an early hymnal *Miriam's Timbrel: Sacred Songs Suited to Revival Occasions; and also for Anti-Slavery, Peace, Temperance and Reform Meetings.* This hymnal consists of songs appropriate for each type of rally, as well as a general section of "Songs for the Reformer." Among the latter the following is typical:

> We will speak out. We will be heard.
>   Though all earth's systems crack.
> We will not bate a single word
>   Nor take a letter back.
>
> We speak the Truth, and what care we
>   For hissing and for scorn
> While some faint gleamings we can see
>   of freedom's coming morn.
>
> Let liars fear; let cowards shrink;
>   Let traitors turn away.
> Whatever we have dared to think
>   that dare we also say.

Wesleyans tested the spirituality of a church by its commitment to reform but refused to substitute reform for piety. Orange Scott warned the young church in 1845 that "deep Experience in the things of God is essential to the peace and usefulness of all Christians; but especially is it essential to any class of Christian Reformers." Wesleyans often spoke of the conjunction of "piety and radicalism," claiming to excel in both areas. The host pastor of the founding convention of the church had tried to assure the early Wesleyans that they would be welcome by affirming that "we believe there is sufficient piety and radicalism to entertain all who will attend."

Another characteristic of the Wesleyans was specificity in their attacks on social evil. Scott insisted that "in opposing sin, the power of the Gospel must be brought to bear upon *particular evils. Generalizing* will not answer. We must *particularize*." And Scott believed in starting at home by attacking "*popular sins* and *sins of the Church*."

The Wesleyans did not center their attack on the South. Scott insisted that "all northern Christians, who neglect to lift up the warning voice and *refuse to take sides* with God's suffering poor, *are scarcely less guilty*." This involved a sense of "corporate guilt" that is made explicit in a statement of George Pegler stating why he left the Methodist Protestants to join the Wesleyans. Though lengthy, its contemporary relevance and contradiction of the stereotypes of pietistic individualism justify more extensive quotation.

> We believe that the churches of the North are responsible for the continuance of slavery. . . .
>
> First, the churches at the North, as well as at the South, hold the slave-holder in Christian fellowship, thus endorsing his Christian character and esteeming him as a brother beloved, and thus justifying his daily acts of man stealing.
>
> Second, by members of the northern churches voting at elections for the man-thief, and his apologist, thus giving evidence that they approve of the wicked laws they enact, whereby they oppress the poor. This is done every year. And the church approves of these acts, and is thus striking hands with the oppressor instead of being a reprover of those who commit the deeds of darkness.
>
> Third, the members of the northern churches sustain those parties that make those civil laws which crush the poor colored man in their midst; and among those who are victims of this cruel class legislation are many who are members of their own church.
>
> Fourth, in most of the churches at the North the "negro pew" is erected, thus showing that they despise the poor, and have "become respectors of persons."
>
> Fifth, but few of the churches at the North will allow their doors to be open to plead the cause of the poor and oppressed. They are willing to hear harangues in praise of Henry Clay, or Martin Van

Buren, or any slave-holder or his apologist, but the man who will dare to open his mouth for the dumb or attempt to exhibit the wickedness and wrongs of slavery will have the door shut in his face; or if he be allowed to speak, his views will be distorted and himself held up to ridicule; or maybe he will be represented as a Traitor to his country, and enemy to republicanism, and often be in personal danger from the fury of a pro-slavery mob, headed by officers and prominent members of a Christian church.

But this emphasis on the role of the Northern churches must not be taken to mean that the Wesleyans were afraid to tackle slavery directly. In 1847 Adam Crooks answered a call to North Carolina. He wrote in his diary, "I turned my face to go to the far south, to pronounce that Gospel which proclaims liberty to the captives, and the opening of the prisons to them that are bound." Such "missionaries" were mobbed, dragged into court, and imprisoned. At least one Wesleyan minister in the South was lynched. But these preachers set about founding churches with such names as Freedom Hill and Lovejoy Memorial Chapel. (Lovejoy was an abolitionist editor killed by a mob wishing to destroy his paper.) Crooks wrote back from the South that "opposition to my course is great. My image was tarred and feathered in this town. . . . [S]ome of my friends are beginning to tremble for my personal safety; but my trust is in the Friend of the poor, the Deliverer of the oppressed." Crooks eventually had to leave the state to escape imprisonment on the charge of

> with force and arms, knowingly, wickedly, and unlawfully, with intention to excite insurrection, conspiracy, and resistance in the slaves and free negroes and persons of color within the state, bringing into the state with the intention to circulate, a printed pamphlet named and styled the "Ten Commandments."

Orange Scott unfortunately met an early death in 1847. There circulates among some Wesleyans today the rumor that on his deathbed Scott renounced his "worldly" reform activities, but his memoirs reveal otherwise. He regretted that his responsibilities in the "book business" had become so consuming. He wished that he had given up that work and carried out his original plans. He regretted that he had not given himself more fully to the oppressed and fought for a reordering of society on their behalf. In his own words,

> I should have gone into the work of impressing on the wealthy classes, their duty to the millions enduring poverty and toil. I feel deeply for that class, and would do my share in carrying forward a practical plan of reform, according to any means. The condition of the masses is wretched indeed, and a great change should be effected in the state of society. It might be done if a few strong men would take hold of it in the pulpit and elsewhere.

Scott's death forced others into leadership of the new denomination. Among these was Luther Lee, who had been born November 30, 1800, into an impoverished upstate New York home. At nineteen Lee reaffirmed the faith of his childhood and, though nearly illiterate, moved toward the Methodist ministry. After several years in frontier circuits and efforts to overcome his lack of education, he rose to leadership, largely because of his powers as a revivalist and his ability in debate. (Lee gained quite a reputation for debating Universalist ministers on the question of universal salvation.)

Luther Lee: abolitionist and feminist; pastor and leader in the Wesleyan Methodist Connection

In 1837 Lee became an abolitionist and immediately threw himself into the antislavery struggle. "Logical Lee," as he came to be called, was especially in demand to defend ministers in church trials for such offenses as "agitating the slavery question" or "patronizing abolitionist publications." After a period of service as an agent of the

Massachusetts Abolition Society and helping to organize the anti-slavery Liberty Party in 1840, Lee joined Orange Scott and others in founding Wesleyan Methodism.

Lee presided over three of the first six General Conferences of the new denomination, edited the *True Wesleyan*, and defended church positions in various writings. He also wrote a number of shorter theological works (attacking Unitarianism and defending the immortality of the soul against "conditionalism," which affirmed that only Christians received immortality) as well as a systematic theology that went through a dozen editions. Lee later served the Wesleyans as professor of theology at Adrian College before returning to the Methodist Episcopal Church after the Civil War.

Lee left behind several volumes of sermons (*The Evangelical Pulpit, 1854–1864*) and a number published in pamphlet form. These materials provide insight into Wesleyan preaching in an era when the social gospel was still a part of evangelicalism.

Lee's understanding of the relationship of preaching to public issues is seen in a late (ca. 1864) sermon titled "The radicalism of the Gospel." There he argued the basic thesis that "THE GOSPEL IS SO RADICALLY REFORMATORY, THAT TO PREACH IT FULLY AND CLEARLY, IS TO ATTACK AND CONDEMN ALL WRONG, AND TO ASSERT AND DEFEND ALL RIGHTEOUSNESS."

Lee defended this position by "denying all neutrality or middle ground" and quoted the words of Jesus: "He that is not with me is against me" (Matt. 12:30). He maintained that the "Gospel asserts its radical reform position, by demanding absolute obedience and submission." Lee opposed all decisions based on "expedience," insisting that "right must be responded to, regardless of worldly considerations." He argued that "ministers, Christians, and churches, lose their moral power when they fail to exemplify the whole gospel." Therefore, "reformers should be reformed," just as "to promote a revival of religion, we must have the elements of a revival in our own breasts."

Lee was certain that "the gospel will never reform mankind, only so far as it is applied specifically to the evils to be removed." This would immediately involve entering the political arena. Lee insisted that "a large portion of the evils are connected with civil government, and the gospel will never remove them, until it is so preached as to have something to do with politics." (On the other hand, Lee insisted in his autobiography that "I never had any politics which were not a part of my religion, and I urged men to vote the Liberty ticket as a religious duty.")

With this background, one can understand the sermons Lee preached in response to some of the great events of his day. Lee himself was radicalized by the death of Rev. Elijah P. Lovejoy, an abolitionist editor shot by a mob trying to silence him by destroying his press for the fourth time. Until this time Lee had assumed that since abolitionists were "attacked by the religious press . . . they must be a set of desperate fanatics." But upon the death of Lovejoy, Lee was "stirred, and judged it wrong to remain silent any longer." As Lee put it later, "I preached a sermon on the death of Mr. Lovejoy, in which I condemned all mob violence, vindicated the principles for the utterance of which Mr. Lovejoy had been killed, and condemned slavery as an unmitigated wrong."

Among other questions, Lee asked, "Suppose the promulgation of Abolition principles does really endanger the slave-holders of the south, where does the fault rest? On the Abolitionist, or on the slave-holding system?" A racist society blamed the abolitionist for tearing it apart. The abolitionists insisted on throwing the blame back onto society and its sins.

A decade later Lee preached another sermon that revealed how much the issues had changed. This sermon was evoked by the death of Rev. Charles Turner Torrey in a Baltimore prison while serving a sentence for invading the South to help slaves escape. Those like Lee who took an active part in the underground railroad had to face the fact, as had Oberlin, that such activities were illegal under the federal Fugitive Slave Laws. And Lee followed the course that Oberlin had taken by developing a doctrine of civil disobedience that appealed to the "higher law."

Lee expressed this position in his sermon titled "The Supremacy of the Divine Law." After urging the right of the slaves to freedom on the basis of the Scriptures and "unalienable rights" (that is, on the basis of the Declaration of Independence), Lee praised Torrey for "placing the law of God and the claims of his Maker above all human law, and the praise or the wrath of men."

Lee also defended Torrey against his more "friendly" detractors. Lee was convinced that "no man can at this day and in this country, rise up and contend for all that is right in politics and religion, and carry out by consistent action the principles for which he contends without being accused of rashness by his opposers, and suspected of indiscretion by his pretended friends."

Again like Oberlin, Lee found that this position pushed him to support John Brown's raid on Harper's Ferry. Brown's action was in effect a form of guerilla warfare—he had hoped that the slaves would rise up and join him in throwing off the yoke of oppression.

Lee responded to Brown's execution by preaching a sermon titled "Dying to the Glory of God." Here again, he appealed both to biblical example and to the precedent of the American Revolution to argue that in some cases "it is right to oppose oppression, and defend human liberty . . . by force and arms." This position amounted to a rationale for a "just revolution" in the face of oppression.

This sermon apparently came to the attention of the family of John Brown, for the following July 4 Lee was invited to deliver another oration from the rock overlooking Brown's grave in North Elba, New York. Lee himself called it "the oration of my life, the most radical and, probably, the most able I ever delivered." Unfortunately this speech did not survive. Lee loaned the manuscript to a reporter and never saw it again.

But another sermon, more than any other, assured Lee of a place in history. Luther Lee preached the ordination sermon for Antoinette Brown, apparently the first woman in history to be fully ordained to the Christian ministry. Rev. Brown was, as has been mentioned, a graduate of Oberlin, where she had also studied theology. Lee had been a major defender of the women delegates who had tried to be seated at various temperance conventions. Antoinette Brown had been among these delegates and apparently asked Lee to preach because of those contacts.

So on September 15, 1853, Luther Lee preached a sermon titled "Woman's Right to Preach the Gospel." He argued exegetically that there was no valid objection to the ordination of women on biblical grounds. This involved a number of steps (making explicit the major roles of women in the New Testament and the early church, arguing that in the relevant Pauline passages, "the apostle's injunction was not given as a general rule, but as a remedy for a specific difficulty," etc.). But the heart of his argument was based on his text (Gal. 3:28—a verse that had been crucial for Lee's antislavery sentiments as well): "There is neither Jew nor Greek, there is neither bond nor free, there is neither male nor female; for ye are all one in Christ Jesus."

It is difficult to know how to evaluate the Wesleyans. How can we put the discussion into contemporary terms? A racist and slaveholding society viewed the abolitionists as insurrectionists. Perhaps that was not inappropriate. Historian Donald G. Matthews suggests that to

> call him a reformer would be to misunderstand his importance; rather, he was a revolutionary. . . . He opposed a whole system. He demanded not the reform of slavery, but its abolition, and in doing so, implied the destruction of Southern and even American society as he and his contemporaries knew it. The implication of the abolitionist preaching was a new kind of society much different from the old—an implication only gradually being realized in the 20th century.[1]

Orange Scott, Luther Lee, and the Wesleyan Methodists have been vindicated in recent years. What appeared as revolution and insurrection to their contemporaries now appears to us to have been responsible social witness. With clear foresight Luther Lee predicted this in his sermon preached on the death of Orange Scott in 1847: "If it be insisted that he was ultra and rash, it was because he lived in advance of his age. He advocated no sentiments, and resorted to no measures, which are not destined, very soon, to become the moderate sober views of the world."

Postscript by Douglas M. Strong

Because Luther Lee believed that the "radicalism of the Gospel" provided Christians with a mandate to "attack and condemn all wrong and to assert and defend all righteousness," he and his fellow Wesleyan

---

1. Donald G. Matthews, "Orange Scott: The Methodist Evangelist as Revolutionary," in *The Anti-Slavery Vanguard: New Essays on the Abolitionists*, ed. Martin Duberman (Princeton: Princeton University Press, 1965), 100.

Methodists supported a range of reform causes such as temperance, women's rights, the democratic restructuring of denominational polity, the abolition of secret societies, the abolition of war, and, of course, the abolition of slavery. In regard to slavery, they were not only opposed to the sin of slaveholding but also resisted the pervasive racial prejudice of the period: in Wesleyan Methodist congregations such as Lee's meetinghouse in Syracuse, all people were welcomed as equals. Lee's church was the only one in the city that did not segregate African Americans who came to worship. Consequently, the church became a haven for fugitive slaves and an important stop along the Underground Railroad.

The Wesleyans' involvement in abolitionism became evident in their sweeping approval for and leadership in the Liberty Party. In their respective periodicals, the *True Wesleyan* and the *Liberty Press*, the denomination publicized the newly established party and the party publicized the fledgling denomination—with affirmative comments in almost every issue of both papers. The editor of the *True Wesleyan* wrote confidently that "in most cases" Wesleyan Methodists were Liberty Party voters. One Wesleyan Methodist member who neglected to vote in the 1844 election felt obliged to print a public apology for his laxity in not promoting the Liberty slate of candidates. The Liberty Party in Vermont was said to have a "predominantly Wesleyan Methodist leadership." Luther Lee argued so forcefully for political action at the 1839 convention where the Liberty Party was formed that he claimed to have "turned the scale in favor of a political antislavery party" and he "boldly urged men to vote for James G. Birney," the Liberty presidential candidate in 1844.

Wesleyans supported the Liberty Party so unabashedly because the party functioned almost like an evangelical institution in which antislavery votes served as evidence of sanctified living. Political abolitionists spoke about a "Liberty Party theology" and affirmed that their ultimate intent was to keep "all men from all sin." Joining the political abolitionist movement represented an individual's "thorough conversion." Just as evangelicals consecrated their lives to Jesus Christ, in like manner, evangelical political abolitionists were urged to "consecrate your votes" to Christ's cause of universal liberty. An antislavery ballot provided proof of a person's unqualified allegiance to God. Abolitionist voting was "the highest moral power we can exercise, as individuals." One Liberty Party–supporting pastor wrote that "we are to be holy always, in all that we do. . . . We are to be as holy . . . in depositing our vote for the election of offices for the state or nation, as in lifting up our hands in prayer to God."

The sanctified ethics of the Liberty Party became tangible in various ways. Unafraid of charges of racial amalgamation, Liberty leaders encouraged African Americans to assume positions of organizational responsibility. Several African Americans, such as Samuel Ringgold Ward, held leadership posts within the party and were nominated by the party to run for political office—an unheard of activity in antebellum America. Unlike other white abolitionists who were against slavery but not concerned with the human dignity of African Americans, many of the white evangelicals in the Liberty Party understood that racial injustice needed to be addressed just as much as legalized servitude. This denunciation of racial exclusion was apparent not only in the way blacks were incorporated but also with the party's proposals to end the Mexican War. The party opposed the war on moral grounds because the war aims notoriously included the enlargement of slave territory and the oppression of Mexicans. Other equal-rights issues championed as ethical imperatives by the Liberty Party encompassed such concerns as homesteading, land-use reform, a progressive income tax, women's suffrage, and opposition to the economic exploitation of Chinese Americans, Native Americans, Irish immigrants, and the industrial working class.[2]

This explicit combination of religious fervor with political rhetoric proved to be controversial in the mid-nineteenth century, and continues to be a contentious topic today. More recent movements on the left, such as the civil rights struggle of the 1950s and '60s, and movements on the right, such as the Moral Majority and Christian Coalition of the 1980s and '90s, have appropriated distinctly religious arguments and phraseology to forward their interests. The question

2. See Douglas M. Strong, *Perfectionist Politics: Abolitionism and the Religious Tensions of American Democracy* (Syracuse: Syracuse University Press, 1999), 67, 84–85, 100–101, 134.

remains of whether such overt expressions of faith in tandem with politics (and vice versa) are appropriate in a pluralistic democratic society. But certainly people of deep religious commitment—like the antebellum Wesleyan Methodists—will persist in their conviction that their relationship with God and obedience to God's will have inescapable implications regarding the outworking of their faith in the public sphere.

8

The Evangelical Roots
of Feminism

The same twists of history that have obscured the evangelical sources of abolitionism have also hidden the early evangelical commitment to feminist principles. By and large, evangelicals were dead set against the 1970s movement of women's liberation. The ordination of women was opposed by the dominant leaders of twentieth-century evangelicalism. Christian bookstores today are filled with innumerable books affirming traditional roles for women, emphasizing the subordination of women to men, and calling evangelical women to a "total" and "fascinating" womanhood that completely submerges their own personalities and aspirations.

Here again, evangelist Billy Graham typified the evangelical attitude of the 1970s. Writing for the *Ladies' Home Journal* he affirmed that "the biological assignment was basic and simple: Eve was to be the child-bearer, and Adam was to be the breadwinner. . . . Wife, mother, homemaker—this is the appointed destiny of real womanhood."[1]

1. Billy Graham, "Jesus and the Liberated Woman," *Ladies' Home Journal*, December 1970, 42.

Similar sentiments were echoed by his wife, Ruth Graham, who responded in the pages of *Christianity Today* to the ordination of women in these words:

> I personally am "agin it." For one thing, I do not feel that we have much of a shortage of men. For another thing, I believe that it basically goes against the principles of Scripture. . . . I think if you study you will find that the finest cooks in the world are men (probably called chefs); the finest couturiers, by and large are men; the greatest politicians are men; most of our greatest writers are men; most of our greatest athletes are men. You name it, men are superior in all but two areas: women make the best wives and women make the best mothers.[2]

The irony of such statements is that modern revivalism gave birth to the women's rights movement. A 1974 anthology of *The Feminist Papers* collected by Alice Rossi began to set the record straight by tracing the roots of American feminism to the revivalism of Charles G. Finney and the reform movements it spawned.[3] This theme was repeated by Beverly Wildung Harrison of Union Theological Seminary in New York, who asserted:

> The fact is that the social origins of the woman's rights movement in America will not be fully or adequately understood, nor the early feminists rightly appreciated, until the connection is duly acknowledged between the woman movement and left-wing Reformation evangelicalism in America. It is to Rossi's credit that she is one of the first contemporary feminists to identify the connection between the Second Great Awakening, in which Charles Finney himself was moved to support women's right to pray and testify, and the woman's rights movement.[4]

Actually, it is evangelicalism that next to Quakerism has given the greatest role to women in the life of the church. This practice crested in nineteenth-century American revivalism but was foreshadowed in

2. Ruth Graham, comment in "Others Say . . ." column, *Christianity Today*, June 6, 1975, 32.

3. Alice Rossi, *The Feminist Papers* (New York: Columbia University Press, 1974), pt. 2.

4. Beverly Wildung Harrison, "The Early Feminists and the Clergy: A Case Study in the Dynamics of Secularization," *Review and Expositor* (Winter 1975): 46.

the Evangelical Revival of the preceding century. The reasons for this are complex, and some have already been suggested. There is an implicit leveling force in vital evangelical religion. Some have even argued that the Evangelical Revival transmitted to English society the radical egalitarian ideas that fomented modern revolutions in other contexts. This leveling impact contributed to the rise of the laity in church life, and in this process, women found new roles earlier denied them, just as laymen were allowed to preach and take other forms of leadership.

The evangelical turn to Christian experience also helped open new vistas for women. Such an emphasis undercut the traditional sources of religious authority—trained clergy, ecclesiastical hierarchies, sacramental systems, and so on. When a high premium was placed on sensitivity to religious growth and personal interaction in small groups, it was discovered that women, though denied formal theological training, had a knack for leadership in such contexts. In fact, women by virtue of their socialization (if not inherent qualities) were more attuned to the emotional and personal factors involved in growth through religious faith development.

There was also a certain innovative and experimental thrust to evangelicalism that found expression in such new and strange practices as "field preaching" in the case of George Whitefield, or in setting hymns to popular and contemporary tunes in the case of the Wesleys. These new practices were justified in part pragmatically by whether they worked or not. Wesley himself, a rigidly conventional Oxford don by nature, despised field preaching until he saw how many were converted by its use. After passing through the trauma of breaking into such new practices, evangelicals were able to look back and see that their resistance had been cultural conditioning rather than some absolute understanding derived from the core of biblical faith.

In this way evangelicals began to experiment with new roles for women in the church. Wesley himself gave approval to a few women preachers by the end of his life. And in America the Great Awakenings so reproduced the same phenomena that by the end of the eighteenth century women preachers had begun to appear in such groups as the Freewill Baptists. Evangelicals did not continue in these practices without testing them against scriptural exegesis, but they found that by approaching the Scriptures with unbiased eyes it became clear that women had played a more significant role in the New Testament church than had previously been assumed, and that a biblical case could be made for giving them more responsibilities in the contemporary church. By the beginning of the nineteenth century new conclusions were being expressed in standard reference works. Adam Clarke's highly influential commentary on the Bible, for example, affirmed of women that "under the blessed spirit of Christianity, they have equal *rights*, equal *privileges*, and equal *blessings*, and let me add, they are equally *useful*."

But it was in the American revivalism of Charles G. Finney that such tendencies began to have wide cultural impact and were transformed into the practice of full ordination for women and a form of Christian and biblical feminism. As already indicated, the most controversial of Finney's "new measures" in his revivals was his encouragement of women to speak and pray in public and mixed meetings. Theodore Weld apparently helped push Finney in this direction. During the week of Weld's conversion in 1825, Weld had encouraged the women to speak, and one night "seven females, a number of them the most influential Christians in the city, confessed their sin in being restrained by their sex and prayed publickly in succession." Finney's own commitment to the practice was revealed in the 1827 New Lebanon Conference called to reconcile Finney with the more conservative revivalists from New England. Though allowing women to speak in public assemblies was the most volatile topic of dissension, Finney refused to back down.

We have already seen how Oberlin College became the first coeducational college in the world and one of the few places encouraging women to get a college education. Asa Mahan, Oberlin's first president, was so proud of this record that he suggested for a tombstone epitaph the one fact that he was "the first man, in the history of the race who conducted women, in connection with members of the opposite sex, through a full course of liberal education, and conferred upon her the high degrees which had hitherto been the exclusive prerogatives of men." Antoinette Brown, the first woman to be ordained, remembered Mahan toward the end of her life as "unusually liberal even for the more liberal men of his day."

Oberlin graduated a number of the leaders of feminism. These women later complained that Oberlin had still been a little stuffy and unwilling to go as far as they wished, but it was in the revivalist context that they first found the door to new vistas slightly ajar. Lucy Stone, Oberlin class of 1847, refused to take her husband's name in marriage and was known as "Mrs. Stone." Her name became an epithet used in derision of the "strange creatures" who broke the social convention. At their wedding, she and her husband Henry Blackwell together signed a protest declaring that their marriage implied "no sanction of, nor promise of voluntary obedience to such of the present laws of marriage, as refuse to recognize the wife as an independent, rational being, while they confer upon the husband an injurious and unnatural superiority, investing him with legal powers which no man should possess." Later in 1870 the same couple founded the *Woman's Journal*, the principal suffragist paper.

But the abolitionist controversy enabled a genuine feminism to emerge. Just as the civil rights movement of the 1960s contributed to the modern reemergence of feminism, in the 1830s abolitionism spawned the women's rights movement. There would seem to be several reasons for this connection. The basic egalitarianism of evangelicalism that supported abolitionism was also extended to women. Those who had mustered the courage to attack one social institution found it easier to attack another. Women who mastered the antislavery argument found unexpected parallels to their own situation. But probably most important for the evangelicals were the parallel problems in the interpretation of Scripture.

The Grimké sisters, Angelina and Sarah, made the initial breakthroughs. Their religious history is complex and still not entirely sorted out. Though usually identified as Quakers, they were originally converted from Southern aristocratic Episcopalianism under the influence of Presbyterian revivalism. They apparently turned to Quakerism because that sect most fully expressed their newfound antislavery sentiments. As we have seen, Angelina later became the wife of Theodore Weld. It was in their work with Weld and the Seventy that the Grimké sisters faced severe opposition from the traditional clergy, who argued against women speaking in public to quash their antislavery agitation. Sarah and Angelina were then forced to defend their work.

Sarah Grimké soon developed her feminist principles in *Letters on the Equality of the Sexes*, originally published in 1837. This work explicitly described parallels between the state of the slave and the condition of women. Sarah Grimké signed her letters "Thine in the bonds of womanhood" and suggested that "the cupidity of man soon led him to regard women as property," pointing out that in some parts of the world women were sold into marriage just as slaves. One letter sketched the laws of the age which left "women very little more liberty, or power in some respects, than the slave." She also claimed that "in all ages and countries, woman has more or less been made a *means* to promote the welfare of man, without regard to her own happiness, and the glory of God, as the end of her creation."

But the argument still turned for evangelicals on biblical interpretation. It was abolitionists who discovered "feminist exegesis." The abolitionists faced conservatives who built a "Bible defense of slavery" on biblical instances of slavery and biblical admonitions to obedience on the part of slaves. Those who mastered Theodore Weld's "Bible argument against slavery" and learned to defend the egalitarian and liberationist "spirit" of the Bible against status quo literal interpretations found that the same arguments could be used in support of the women's movement. Even Galatians 3:28 seemed to conjoin the issues by declaring, "There is neither Jew nor Greek, there is neither bond nor free, there is neither male nor female: for ye are all one in Christ Jesus."

The full hermeneutical and theological significance of these moves was not spelled out until later in the century, but the Grimké sisters began immediately to push for more appropriate translations of the Scriptures, pointing out that men had often unconsciously imported sexist distortions into their work. Of the New Testament Sarah insisted, "I am willing to abide by its decision, and must enter my protest against the false translations of some passages by the MEN who did that work. . . . When we are admitted to the honor of studying Greek and Hebrew, we shall produce some versions of the Bible, a little different from those we have now." Illustrative of the kind of retranslation she called for is her comment on the early chapters of Genesis. "The literal translation of the word 'help-meet' is a helper like unto himself; and is so rendered in the Septuagint and manifestly signifies a companion."

Out of these currents flowed a stream of feminism that engulfed much of evangelicalism by the end of the century. In the first generation or so, feminism was found largely in those groups that had been most firmly committed to abolitionism, but by the second generation such convictions had gained a momentum of their own that went beyond the circles that remembered the antislavery struggle.

The Wesleyan Methodists, for example, had striking connections with the women's rights movement. The Seneca Falls meeting of 1848 that launched the movement and first called for the franchise for women was held in a Wesleyan Methodist church—apparently because only the abolitionist denomination was at all receptive to such radical ideas. (Even here there was some equivocation. When the women arrived for the meeting, they found the building locked and had to climb in through a window!) We have already mentioned that Luther Lee of the Wesleyans preached the ordination sermon for Antoinette Brown, the first woman to be fully ordained—even though she was a Congregationalist. Lee appears regularly in the literature of the movement for his efforts to defend women who attempted to attend temperance conventions as full voting delegates.

The convictions that Lee expressed in the ordination sermon, titled "Woman's Right to Preach the Gospel," can only be called feminist. Interpreting Galatians 3:28, he insisted that "I cannot see how the text can be explained so as to exclude females from any right, office, work, privilege, or immunity which males enjoy, hold or perform. If the text means anything, it means that males and females are equal in rights, privileges and responsibilities upon the Christian Platform." In the next decade (the 1860s) some Wesleyan Methodists began to ordain women, nearly a century in advance of the Methodist Episcopal Church. The practice was debated for the rest of the century before becoming relatively common among Wesleyan Methodists in the early years of the twentieth century.

Though he did not speak much on the issue, Presbyterian/Congregationalist Jonathan Blanchard of Wheaton College seems to have shared some of these feminist convictions. In his Cincinnati debate with N. L. Rice, he proclaimed that "the first alteration which Christianity made in the polity of Judaism was to abrogate this oppressive distinction of sexes" in which "women had almost no rights; they were menials to their husbands and parents."

Blanchard and Lee both seem to have preserved the teaching that "the husband is the head of the wife," but others went beyond this to advocate an egalitarian marriage relationship. Among these was B. T. Roberts, founder of the Free Methodist Church, another split from the Methodist Episcopal Church over, at least in part, the question of slavery. Though his denomination did not capitulate to the full ordination of women until 1974 (a fact he profoundly regretted), in 1891 Roberts authored one of the most radical of the evangelical defenses of feminism. In marriage Roberts urged the model of the business partnership:

> The greatest domestic happiness always exists where husband and wife live together on terms of equality. Two men, having individual interests, united only by business ties, daily associate as partners for years, without either of them being in subjection to the other. They consider each other as equals. Then, cannot a man and woman, united in conjugal love, the strongest tie that can unite two human beings having *the same* interests, live together in the same manner?

Roberts's book also explicitly dealt with the hermeneutical issues involved in a "biblical feminism" and argued the parallel with the problem of slavery.

Another Free Methodist bishop, W. A. Sellew, pursued the same issues in *Why Not?* (1894). He claimed that "women the world over have been patiently waiting . . . for the glorious gospel of love, as taught by Jesus Christ and its attendant civilization, to restore to her those rights which have been taken from her by force." He also advocated laws "permitting her to earn and own property and manage her personal business affairs untrammelled by a class of men who think they possess superior knowledge on how a woman's money should be spent."

Baptist A. J. Gordon provides an interesting variation on these themes. Gordon was the major figure behind what has developed into Gordon College and Gordon-Conwell Theological Seminary, the major evangelical educational institutions in New England. His son and biographer indicates that Gordon had "been bred in the strictest sect of the abolitionists" and with regard to women "advocated their complete enfranchisement and their entrance into every political and social privilege enjoyed by men."

When conservatives objected to women speaking at missionary conventions, Gordon responded in an essay titled "The Ministry of Women" in the *Missionary Review of the World* (1894). There he argued that "in every great spiritual awakening in the history of Protestantism the impulse for Christian women to pray and witness for Christ in the public assembly has been found irrepressible." Gordon's essay is largely exegetical in character, but he argued more from Acts 2 than from the usual text of Galatians 3:28. Particular weight was given to a quotation from the Old Testament book of Joel (2:28) to the effect that, in the last days, says God, "I will pour out my Spirit upon all flesh; and your sons *and your daughters* shall prophecy."

A 1970s study uncovered a major role of women in the early years of the Evangelical Free Church, a Scandinavian immigrant denomination formed in the late nineteenth century, known today primarily through its seminary, Trinity Evangelical Divinity School, one of the largest and most prominent of the evangelical seminaries. In a widely distributed pamphlet titled "The Prophesying Daughters," Fredrick Franson, an early leader of the movement and founder of The Evangelical Alliance Mission (TEAM), defended the right of women to preach. In the early years of the church a number of women served not only as traveling evangelists but also as stationed pastors. Full ordination of women was clearly intended in early constitutions, and the 1925 rules for ordination utilized such nonsexist phraseology as "a candidate for ordination shall request a reference from the church of which he or she is a member relative to the candidate's character, abilities, training and anything that pertains to his or her call." The first women to avail themselves of this opportunity included Christina

Carlson, Ellen Modin, Amanda Nelson, Carrie Norgaard, Hilma Severin, and Amanda Gustafson.

But it was the Salvation Army that made the most progress in putting such convictions into practice. This was due to the influence of Catherine Mumford Booth, cofounder of the Army, though many historians hardly mention her. Catherine had at one point nearly refused to marry William Booth when he remarked in a letter that "woman has a fibre more in the heart and a cell less in the brain." She insisted that lack of training and opportunity were solely responsible for woman's secondary place in society, and finally agreed to marriage only after William had accepted feminist convictions.

Catherine entered the fray over "women preachers" in the 1850s, writing letters to church papers and authoring a thirty-two-page pamphlet titled "Female Ministry" that had several editions. She too argued from Pentecost that "the Spirit was given to the female as to the male disciple. . . . [W]hat a remarkable device of the devil that he has succeeded in hiding this, . . . but the time of her deliverance draweth nigh," and lamented that "it is impossible to estimate the extent of the church's loss, where prejudice and custom are allowed to render the outpouring of God's spirit upon His handmaidens null and void."

When William became sick, Catherine substituted for him in the pulpit and soon developed an important preaching ministry of her own. Most reports suggest that she was better in the pulpit than her husband. Often they would split up to "double their power for good" and hold simultaneous preaching missions. In Portsmouth crowds averaging one thousand people came nightly for seventeen weeks to hear her preach, and she often spoke to much larger meetings.

When she had children, Catherine was careful to encourage enlightened attitudes concerning women's roles. "I have tried to grind it into my boys that their sisters were just as intelligent and capable as themselves. Jesus Christ's principles were to put woman on the same platform as men, although I am sorry to say His apostles did not always act upon it." When her daughters were grown and married, they kept the Booth family name by hyphenating it to form Booth-Tucker, Booth-Clibborn, and so on. With such convictions motivating the Salvation Army, it is little wonder that egalitarian principles were built into the structure of the Army from the beginning and that in 1934 Evangeline Booth was elected to the highest office of the Army, that of general.

Nineteenth-century evangelical literature contains intimations of other radical ideas now coming into their own. A. B. Simpson, founder of the Christian and Missionary Alliance, rejected the idea that Christ's incarnation was as a male. In *Echoes of the New Creation* he argued that "His humanity was unique and different from all other humanity. He is not a man, but He is *the* Man. He is not a male. He is just as much a woman as He is a man."

Others suggested the use of female imagery to describe God. Among these was Hannah Whitall Smith, author of the widely read religious classic

Catherine Booth: co-founder of the Salvation Army.

The Christian's Secret of a Happy Life. "H.W.S." was a popular Bible teacher and with her husband, Robert, was a major force behind British Keswick Conventions calling Christians to a deeper spiritual life. She was also a frequent speaker at suffrage conventions and an ardent advocate of women's education. One of her Bible studies in *The Open Secret* is titled "God As Our Mother." In this study she analyzed the "many . . . ways in which God is like a mother" in order to "open our eyes to see some truths concerning Him, which have been hitherto hidden from our gaze."

One cannot discuss evangelical feminism without taking note of Frances Willard, a Methodist crusader who used the Women's Christian Temperance Union to provide a political outlet for women and to fight for the franchise. It was perhaps Willard rather than more radical feminists who made suffrage palatable to the masses by tying the issue into "temperance" and "home protection." But Willard also argued for the ordination of women in *Woman in the Pulpit* (1888) and called for sexually inclusive language in worship, complaining that "preachers almost never refer to the women of their audiences, but tell about 'men' and what 'a man' was and is and is to be."

Phoebe Palmer: leading Holiness speaker and evangelist; advocate for women's right to preach

Similar convictions and practices appear in other evangelical traditions. Lee Anna Starr, Methodist Protestant pastor at Adrian College, authored *The Bible Status of Woman* (1926), a painstaking analysis of the relevant biblical texts. This book was published by Revell, the evangelical publisher associated with the Moody revivals. Methodist medical doctor and reformer Katherine Bushnell spent the latter years of her life working in the original languages to produce books and pamphlets vindicating the Scriptures and defending feminism. Pentecostal traditions boast the ministries of Mary Woodworth-Etter, whom some now consider a founder of Pentecostalism, and Aimee Semple McPherson, founder of the International Church of the Foursquare Gospel.

But it was, however, the denominations produced by the mid-nineteenth-century "holiness revival" that most consistently raised feminism to a central principle of church life. This movement largely emerged from the work of Methodist lay evangelist Phoebe Palmer.

This neglected figure played a major role in the revival of 1857–58 and its extension to the old world by four years of evangelism in the British Isles. But in the midst of these revival efforts she published a 421-page defense of the right of women to preach titled *The Promise of the Father*. This work argued from the account of Pentecost and became the fountainhead of innumerable such arguments developed through the remainder of the nineteenth century and into the twentieth.

Nor was Palmer the only woman evangelist in the formative years of the movement. Another neglected figure is the black ex-slave Amanda Berry Smith, who preached around the world. Methodist Episcopal bishop J. M. Thoburn said of her work in India that "during the seventeen years that I have lived in Calcutta, I have known many famous strangers to visit the city, but I have never known anyone who

Amanda Berry Smith: globe-trotting evangelist and social reform advocate

could draw and hold so large an audience as Mrs. Smith." And of her personal impact on himself he commented, "I have learned more that has been of actual value to me as a preacher of Christian Truth from Amanda Smith than from any other person I have ever met."

The major organ of this movement, the *Guide to Holiness*, frequently considered the role of women in the church. Among the convictions upheld in its pages were: "Pentecost laid the axe at the root of social injustice. The text of Peter's sermon that marvelous day was the keynote of woman's enfranchisement." Objecting to the fact that woman "contents herself with shining, like the moon, with borrowed splendor, as the mother, sister, or wife of the great so-and-so. . . . She has left her talent in its napkin while she has been obeying the world's dictum by helping to make the most of his." "When the Pentecostal light shines most brightly, women do the bulk of the common-school teaching. They are also principals, professors, college presidents, and are admitted to all the learned professions. . . . When the light shines clearly, they have equal rights with men by whose side they labor for God's glory."

With such sentiments in the early years of the Holiness movement, it is not surprising that the "Holiness" denominations that formed later at the turn of the century institutionalized feminist principles. The Church of God (Anderson, Indiana) emerged in the 1880s, and in early years perhaps 20 to 25 percent of ministers and delegates were women. John Smith, historian of the movement, has claimed that "forty years before the time of woman's suffrage on a national level, a great company of women were preaching, singing, writing, and helping to determine the policies in this religious reform movement," and that, "it is probably safe to say that no other movement, either religious or secular, in this period of American history, except the suffrage movement itself, had such a high percentage of women leaders whose contribution was so outstanding."

The major product of the Holiness revival was the Church of the Nazarene, whose 1894 founding constitution specifically provided for the right of women to preach. One entire conference from west Tennessee consisted for a time of only women ministers. Out of the Church of the Nazarene came in 1905 a book titled *Women Preachers* that recorded the testimonies and "calls to ministry" of a dozen such women. Early rolls of Nazarene ministers indicate that perhaps 20 percent of the clergy in this denomination were women.

The Pilgrim Holiness Church was similar. Founder Seth Cook Rees (father of Paul S. Rees, prominent in the founding of the National Association of Evangelicals in the 1940s) worked with his wife as co-pastor and coevangelist. In setting forth his vision for the new church, Rees exploded, "Nothing but jealousy, prejudice, bigotry, and a stingy love for bossing in men have prevented woman's public recognition by the church." An early edition of the Pilgrim Holiness *Manual* indicates that in some sections of the church as many as 30 percent of the ordained ministers were women.

And the more sectarian the body, the firmer its feminist convictions. The most striking illustration of this is a minuscule Holiness denomination called the Pillar of Fire. This group was founded by Alma White, wife of a Methodist minister. This woman was consecrated a bishop by her denomination, and she claimed to be the first woman bishop in Christian history. Even more interesting, for years this denomination published under the editorship of Mrs. White a paper called *Woman's Chains*, calling for the complete enfranchisement of women, their functioning in Congress and the presidency, and other forms of complete equality in both church and society.

Such were the feminist convictions of large sections of what has come to be known as evangelicalism. This heritage is almost totally lost today except where it was more firmly institutionalized, such as in the Salvation Army. Even those denominations most firmly committed to women in the ministry have largely abandoned the practice. By 1973 the percentage of women ministers in the Church of the Nazarene had dropped to about 6 percent. What was no doubt the most massive effort to incorporate women into the life of the Christian church has faded away and today is not even remembered.

9

Anointed to Preach the Gospel to the Poor

The Civil War marks a major point of transition in the evangelical social consciousness. Some of the social and theological reasons for the shifts that took place will be developed in the next chapter. Here it is sufficient to note that pre–Civil War revivalism tended to split into two streams. On the more liberal side was the social gospel movement, in which persons like Walter Rauschenbusch emerged from revivalism to apply Christian principles to labor relations, urbanization, and so forth. Timothy Smith has argued in his still controversial book *Revivalism and Social Reform*[1] that the social gospel had strong roots in pre–Civil War revivalism and carried into the postwar era the broader themes of progress and hope for a Christian society. Whatever the validity of his thesis, it is the social gospel movement that has received the most attention from historians of the late nineteenth century. It has generally been assumed that the increasing polarizations

---

1. Timothy L. Smith, *Revivalism and Social Reform in Mid-nineteenth Century America* (New York: Abingdon, 1957), esp. chap. 14.

within Protestantism that climaxed in the fundamentalist/modernist controversy of the 1920s and '30s forced a split between those with a "social conscience" and those who advocated a "personal gospel" of individual regeneration.

This caricature contains some truth, but it is also a grave distortion. Just as the social gospel was a manifestation of a social conscience among theological liberals, there was also a disaffection with bourgeois church life among the more theologically conservative. This movement (in some ways more conservative and in some ways more radical than the social gospel) drew its inspiration even more clearly from Finney's "new measure" revivalism. This little-known aspect of American church life cries out for further study, not only to fill out the history of the period but also for the illumination of current questions. This chapter can only provide hints of the material available for study.

Historians have wondered what happened to the abolitionist impulse after the Civil War. To some extent it died out with the emancipation of the slaves, though many Christians, sensitive to the broader problems of prejudice and injustice, devoted their lives to work among the freedmen. But the major force of the antislavery struggle was in the postwar era rechanneled into the "purity crusade" against prostitution. This movement captured the major figures in the antislavery struggle (from William Lloyd Garrison on down the line) and the rhetoric that had been used against slavery. Now the goal was to "abolish" (rather than regulate!) the "white slave trade" that supported the widespread prostitution of the era.

This purity crusade was closely tied to another issue held over from the pre–Civil War period—temperance reform. Here, too, the aim was not regulation but abolition—total abstinence and prohibition. Modern sympathy has been more with the antislavery struggle, which in a sense succeeded, than with the movement for prohibition, which was eventually rejected. This fact has obscured the character of temperance reform and its real parallels with the antislavery movement. Both campaigns sought a major restructuring of society. In the debate between "personal regeneration" and "cleaning up the environment" as approaches to moral and social rehabilitation, the temperance movement came out on the liberal side. It called for altering the environment so that people would not be subjected to the social problems attributed to alcohol.

But it is true that the purity crusade and the temperance movement were more amenable to a "personal morality" orientation. While the slaveholder was the sinner in the case of slavery, the prostitute and the drunkard were more directly engaged in sin and needed to be "rescued" from their plight. In these movements the broader social issues did drop into the background, though as we shall see this was not the whole story.

The purity crusade and temperance reform were at the time expressions of real concern for the outcasts of society. In this work evangelicals in part acted in obedience to and in part discovered a basic affirmation of Scripture that is only now being reemphasized by the church. If there is a consistent theme in the activist movements in the church, from liberation theology to more traditional belief, it is the declaration for a special Christian responsibility to the poor and oppressed of this world. These movements proclaim that the Scriptures have a bias in favor of the economically poor. This concern is clear in the Gospel of Luke, where Jesus quotes the prophet Isaiah to describe his own mission as being "anointed to preach the gospel to the poor" (Luke 4:18). The rest of the Gospel of Luke makes it clear that "poor" must be understood primarily in economic terms.

This theme appears regularly in the theologically conservative disaffection from bourgeois church life in the late nineteenth century. These evangelicals understood this biblical teaching and gave themselves to the poor and the inner cities in response. This impulse was clearly grounded in the work of Finney and his friends. We have already seen (in chap. 6) how the New York churches under Finney's influence belonged to a separate Third Presbytery that consisted only of "free churches." These churches were so called because they were a self-conscious protest against the "renting" or selling of pews, a practice that grew in some circles as churches moved into the middle and upper classes and began to build more elaborate sanctuaries, in some cases modeled on a small scale on European cathedrals.

The Finneyites resisted this practice. Such rentals encouraged seating according to wealth and social class and thereby contradicted scriptural injunctions about being a "respecter of persons." Though some pews were usually left unassigned, to sit there was a sign of poverty and a public embarrassment that discouraged the poor from attending church and contributed to alienation between social classes. This practice seemed inconsistent with the teachings of Jesus that the church has a special responsibility to the poor.

The question of "free churches" continued to be a matter of contention in a variety of denominations in the middle decades of the nineteenth century. Usually the struggle was contained within each denomination, with some churches insisting on "free seats" while others adopted a rental system. But in at least one case these questions made a major contribution to the emergence of a new denomination. In 1860 tensions in upstate New York led to the founding of the Free Methodist Church. The word "free" stood for a number of things, including abolitionism and the principle of "free pews."

The struggle over this issue was intense in the Methodist Episcopal Church, which, though it had been primarily a lower-class or lower-middle-class church, was now rapidly rising into the upper-middle class. The principle of "free seats" had been written into the Methodist Episcopal *Discipline* as follows: "Let all our churches be built plain and decent, and with free seats; but not more expensive than is absolutely unavoidable; otherwise the necessity of raising money will make rich men necessary to us. But if so, we must be dependent on them, yea, and governed by them. And then farewell to Methodist discipline, if not doctrine too."

But this rule was dropped in 1852, and the way was opened for the pew-rental system to be introduced into Methodism. In response to this decision and its broader implications for church life, the Free Methodist Church was born. A statement in an early *Discipline* of this group embedded this principle of "free seats" into the basic statement of purpose. "All their churches are required to be as free as the grace they preach. They believe that their mission is two-fold—to maintain the Bible standard of Christianity—and to preach the Gospel to the poor. Hence they require that all seats in their houses of worship should *be free*."

The rest of this statement was taken from an article in the first issue of the *Earnest Christian*, edited by B. T. Roberts, founder of the denomination. In that editorial Roberts expresses his understanding of the class bias of the Scripture and appeals to the Lukan texts so popular today.

B. T. Roberts: founder of the Free Methodist Church and advocate for women's ordination

> The provisions of the Gospel are for all. . . . *But for whose benefit are special efforts to be put forth?* Who must be *particularly* cared for? Jesus settles this question. He leaves no room for cavil. When John sent to know who he was, Christ charged the messengers to return and show John the things which they had seen and heard. "The blind receive their sight, and the lame walk; the lepers are cleansed, and the deaf hear; the dead are raised up," and, as if all this would be insufficient to satisfy John of his claims, he adds, "AND THE POOR HAVE THE GOSPEL PREACHED TO THEM." This was the crowning proof that He was the ONE THAT SHOULD COME.

Roberts insisted that "in this respect the Church must follow in the footsteps of Jesus. She must see that the gospel is preached to the poor." He also came very close to arguing that obedience to this example is *the* sign of the true church. "There are hot controversies about the true church. . . . It may be that there cannot be church without a bishop, or that there can. There can be none without a gospel, and a gospel for the poor." Or again, "the poor are the favored ones. They are not called up. The great are called down."

The Free Methodists made this the determinative principle for the whole of church life. Roberts argued that "the edifice in which the gospel is preached should be built plain, and with all the seats free, with special reference to meeting the needs of the poor." Similarly, "the Free Methodist church requires all its members to dress plain. So plain people need not be afraid to attend church with them." Roberts pushed his followers to a radical discipleship that affirmed a simple lifestyle, polemicized against the "modern, easy way of getting people converted, without repentance, without renouncing the world," and insisted that such renunciation of the world include such social sins as "slavery, driving hard bargains, and oppressing the hireling in his wages."

As the century wore on, such convictions became more widespread among evangelicals. With the growth of cities, "preaching the gospel to the poor" involved a call to the inner-city districts and, more explicitly, to ministry in skid row and red-light districts. A. B. Simpson, who came to New York's 13th Street Presbyterian Church in 1879, struggled for two years to turn this church outside itself to the poor of New York City and described the increasing polarization in these words: "What they wanted was a conventional parish for respectable Christians. What this young pastor wanted was a multitude of publicans and sinners."

Finally Simpson resigned, announcing his decision in an address based on the text "the Spirit of the Lord is upon me because he hath anointed me to preach the gospel to the poor." He then began a series of moves around the city that climaxed in founding the "Gospel Tabernacle" for immigrants located in the Times Square area. Out of Simpson's work grew the Christian and Missionary Alliance, a movement that originally understood itself to have a special call to serve the "neglected classes both at home and abroad."

The Church of the Nazarene was an interdenominational movement that brought together a number of people who shared the belief that it was the Christian's responsibility to minister to the poor. After years of service in some of the most beautiful churches and well-paid pulpits of California Methodism, Phineas F. Bresee felt called in the 1890s into ministry to the poor of inner-city Los Angeles. Bresee originally hoped to maintain his ministerial relationship in the Methodist conference while engaging in this work, but the bishop and his cabinet refused this request, forcing him to sever his lifelong relationship to found in 1895 the Church of the Nazarene.

The original "Articles of Faith and General Rules" described the "field of labor" of the new church as "the neglected quarters of the cities." The name Church of the Nazarene was chosen to symbolize "the toiling, lowly mission of Christ" by taking a "name which was used in derision of Him by His enemies." Like their predecessors in this succession, the Nazarenes adapted the whole of their church life to this mission. They objected to the wealth spent in elaborate churches, not only because such churches made the poor feel uncomfortable, but because the money used should have been spent to feed and clothe the hungry and the naked.

Illustrative of these sentiments is the following statement: "We want places so plain that every board will say welcome to the poorest. We can get along without rich people, but not without preaching the gospel to the poor. . . . Let the Church of the Nazarene be true to its commission; not great and elegant buildings; but to feed the hungry and clothe the naked, and wipe away the tears of sorrowing; and gather jewels for His diadem."

But such sentiments were not just Bresee's. Large parts of the denomination in the Southwest consisted of little more than chains of inner-city missions. One paper, started in 1906 in Texas, was called *Highways and Hedges*. Its title boldly proclaimed that "the respectable have had this call and rushed madly on after

Phineas Bresee: founder of the Church of the Nazarene; developed ministry with the poor

the things of this world" and claimed that "Steeple-house church people are busy chasing dollars . . . while some are too firmly married to their church creeds to listen to the call." This paper vowed to "open up a chain of missions in all of our large cities where real

mission and slum work will be pushed; and the poor and the des-
titute looked after."

Similar convictions were echoed by A. M. Hills, the first systematic
theologian of the new denomination. In preaching a sermon on "He
Hath Anointed Me" from Luke 4:18–19, Hills said Jesus

> was anointed to preach good tidings to the poor. An English writer has
> said that the oppression of the poor by the rich and powerful and their
> patience under oppressions and wrongs is ever the marvel of history.
> The poor were never appreciated until Christ came. . . . In the eyes of
> Christian law and of our country all men are on a common footing
> of rights and equality whatever their condition. Why? Because Jesus
> came to the poor, to preach the gospel to them, to tell them of their
> worth as men regardless of all accidents of birth, position, or race.

While groups like the Church of the Nazarene were in the beginning primarily a chain of rescue missions, this work did not always
produce new denominations. Some institutions were supported by
denominations as a part of their work in the inner cities, and other
missions, like the famous Pacific Garden Mission in Chicago, were
denominationally independent, deriving support from a number
of sources. Usually such missions were located in skid-row areas
and focused on the down-and-out alcoholic, providing meals, lodg-
ing, clothing, medical care, efforts at rehabilitation, and of course
"salvation."

The origins of this movement are obscure, though there were antecedents in Europe, particularly in the work of Thomas Chalmers.
But the earliest in America was a small mission with a single room
in the Five Points district of Manhattan. Very often such institutions
provided an outlet for women not able to minister in normal churches.
This mission was started by a group of Methodist women, including
evangelist Phoebe Palmer, who "were attracted to this place accompanied with an earnest desire to test the power of Christianity to
give life even there." Their work was not without opposition. "They
were told by gentlemen whom they requested to survey the ground,
that no suitable room could be procured, but they expressed their
determination to send a missionary there, which they did in 1850."

These women later raised money to buy an "Old Brewery," which was demolished for the building of a new "mission house." This mission worked with children as well as adults, holding several kinds of meetings and Sunday schools. Temperance societies were founded, and efforts were made to find employment. Plans were announced to build housing, to establish a hospital, to generate employment, and in other ways to serve the needs of this community.

But the most famous of the early rescue missions was the Water Street Mission, which was founded in 1872 by ex-convict Jerry McAuley and which became the model for scores of similar institutions around the world. Converted in the Water Street Mission was S. H. Hadley, the dominant figure in the movement. A. T. Pierson claimed that perhaps seventy-five thousand men were converted under Hadley's influence. Hadley's brother was also converted at the Water Street Mission and went on to found more than sixty rescue missions himself. Through these missions the evangelical world of the age launched a major war against liquor.

Parallel to these rescue missions for men were institutions committed to work among "fallen women." Emma Whittemore founded the first Door of Hope in 1890, some fifteen years after being converted under the influence of Jerry McAuley at the Water Street Mission. Before Whittemore's death, one hundred homes had been opened.

Similarly, in 1882 after the death of his five-year-old daughter, Charles Crittenton turned to such work and plowed into it the fortune he had made in the drug business. He named his missions the Florence Crittenton homes after his daughter, and the chain grew to some seventy-five. This was not easy work. The churches looked down on him for involving himself with such "unsavory" people, and much time had to be spent convincing respectable church people that women were often involved in prostitution out of economic necessity and kept in it because no one would help them get out or get jobs.

Many other manifestations of these themes could be mentioned, but their profoundest incarnation was the Salvation Army. This movement originated in England as the Christian Mission founded in the 1860s by William and Catherine Booth. This mission was a protest against "respectable churches" whose life cut them off from the masses. Its dominant concern was to follow Christ, "who, though he was rich, yet for our sakes became poor, that we, through his poverty, might become rich, and who has left us an example that we should follow in his steps."

The Salvation Army came to America about 1880 and by the end of the century had thousands of officers engaged in relief and evangelism throughout the cities of the world. A living critique of the bourgeois churches and a disturber of the peace by revealing the sickening underside of a supposedly respectable society, the Army generated intense opposition from both mobs and church people. In one twelve-month period about 1880, 669 Salvationists were reported "knocked down, kicked, or brutally assaulted," 56 army buildings were stormed, and 86 Salvationists imprisoned (the mobs attacked, but the Salvationists were arrested and imprisoned).

Though primarily concerned with salvation and preaching the gospel to the poor, the Salvation Army, like other slum workers, soon found itself providing other services. Most immediate were the needs for food, clothing, and shelter. A "poor man's bank" was established. Day-care centers were provided to permit mothers to get out to earn a living for their families. The Army discovered that the legal system was biased toward those who could afford to hire counsel, and it therefore provided free legal aid. Special attention was given to work among prisoners. The Army sought to become the custodian of first offenders to prevent their being sent to prisons that would turn them into hardened criminals. (Other work among prisoners yielded some unexpected dividends; one Army post in 1896 reported that forty-seven of its forty-eight members had prison records!)

Prostitution was a particular concern of the Army. The Booths startled many with sympathy for the prostitute, arguing that social conditions, more than inherent evil, forced young women into the "world's oldest profession." The Booths joined forces with muckraking journalist W. T. Stead to expose the white slave trade in which young girls were kidnapped, tricked, or sold into prostitution. Stead arranged for the purchase of a young virgin and wrote up the incident in his paper. The controversy resulted in Stead's imprisonment but forced Parliament to provide a legal weapon against the practice by raising the age of consent.

Stead carried this campaign to America and in 1894 published a book titled *If Christ Came to Chicago*. This book must rank as a classic of Christian "investigative reporting." It named names and marshaled devastating facts and statistics. One appendix contained a "black list" that indicated not only the ostensible owner of each building in Chicago's red-light district, but also who really paid the taxes. The result was a major shake-up in Chicago.

The work of Stead and the Salvation Army shows the inadequacy of viewing these movements as conservative because they emphasized conversion. They incarnated egalitarian ideas about women, for example, far in advance of their age and provided in many cases an outlet for church women denied access to other roles of ministry. These movements explicitly rejected the double standard of sexual ethics and generated sympathy for the exploited prostitute. Their work did much to contribute to the "discovery of poverty" in the late nineteenth century that supported the "progressive reforms." Personal understanding of the conditions in the slums provided the basis for the support of new legislation.

But even more striking is that close contact with the poor and oppressed forced Salvationists and other slum workers into an increasingly radical critique of American society. The Booths' son Ballington argued that "we must have justice—more justice . . . to right the social wrong by charity is like bailing the ocean with a thimble. . . . We must adjust our social machinery so that the producers of wealth become the owners of wealth." In a biography of Catherine Booth, W. T. Stead called her a "Socialist, and something more" because she was "in complete revolt against the existing order." And the Army's primary organ, the *War Cry*, asserted that the chief social evil in America was the "unequal and unjust distribution of wealth."

The Booths followed closely the emergence of socialism and related utopian visions and strongly affirmed elements of both. As William Booth put it, "I say nothing against any short cut to the Millennium that is compatible with the Ten Commandments. I intensely sympathize with the aspirations that lie behind all these socialist dreams. . . . [W]hat these good people want to do, I also want to do." But he feared that many schemes were idealistic and

actually avoided the immediate pressing needs of the poor. He drew
an interesting parallel with certain forms of Christian theology.

> This religious cant which rids itself of all the importunity of suffering
> humanity by drawing unnegotiable bills payable on the other side of
> the grave is not more impracticable than the socialist clap-trap which
> postpones all redress of human suffering until after the general overturn.
> Both take refuge in the Future to escape a solution of the problems of the
> Present, and it matters little to the sufferers whether the Future is on this
> side of the grave or the other. Both are for them, equally out of reach.

The adequacy of that pragmatic turn of mind I shall leave to others
to debate. The point here is to draw attention to a certain evangelical
protest against the bourgeois church of the late nineteenth century.
This protest drew its inspiration from Christ's mission of "preaching
the gospel to the poor." Obedience to that ideal forced those who
followed it not only into various forms of social service and welfare
work, but also to profound identification with the class interests of
the poor and a consequent radical critique of existing society.

Postscript by Douglas M. Strong

Nineteenth-century evangelicals became anxious about the economic
direction taken by American society. Expanding commercialization
led entrepreneurs away from local markets and toward consolidation
with the broader, urbanizing culture. In 1862, the Methodist Episcopal
preacher Peter Cartwright visited New York City and censured it for
its "blind money-madness." The same transportation technology that
encouraged prosperity and the spread of the gospel also encouraged
economic displacement and the spread of unsanctified patterns of
behavior. Wesleyan Methodists lamented "the increasing desecration
of the Holy Sabbath, especially along canals, railroads, and thor-
oughfares throughout this nation—thus turning these improvements
into curses."[2] The emerging consumer-oriented culture led to moral

2. Stanley W. Wright, *One Hundred Years of Service for Christ in the Wesleyan
Methodist Church, 1844–1944* (E. R. Philo Company, Elmira, NY, 1944), 17.

compromise among affluent Christians and created urban slums in which poorer people had no recourse or safety net.

Evangelicals responded to the effects of these economic dislocations in various ways. By recognizing that alcoholism exacerbated the social problems of city life, for instance, some evangelicals came to think that the damage perpetrated by strong drink represented the greatest threat to holiness in the economically expanding United States. Reducing or even banning alcohol use became a simple tactic through which some Christians hoped a converted America could overcome its bourgeois excess. At times, the temperance crusade functioned in a patronizing way as a Victorian means of trying to control the working class through their personal self-mastery of destructive habits. But in addition to the tendency to assert social control and individual morality, the temperance movement also addressed larger structural issues in American society. The promotion of temperance highlighted the deep-seated systemic effects of alcohol, especially among men who often got drunk and then abused their wives and children. As we have seen, then, women were often in the forefront of this reform movement, especially through organizations such as the Women's Christian Temperance Union, and temperance activity often led evangelical women to advocate for their rights, including suffrage.

Another response to the economic challenges of the nineteenth century was evangelicals' disaffection with the middle-class craving for wealth and respectability. As mentioned above, Oberlinites and Free Methodists attacked pew rentals because the practice heightened class and race distinctions and discouraged the poor from attending church. The work of the Salvation Army, the Church of the Nazarene, and others involved in inner-city missions caused them to identify with the interests of the disenfranchised and to offer a critique of existing society. The social-reform heritage of the Holiness and early Pentecostal movements opposed many aspects of the modernizing paradigm. They impugned the dominant consumer-driven, patriarchal, racialized mind-set of the period.

When African American pastor Samuel Ringgold Ward wrote about the unusual degree of affirmation he received from the all-white congregation he served in South Butler, New York, in the 1840s, he was convinced that their unprejudiced behavior was due to the fact that they lived "apart from the allurements and deceptions of fashion, [where] they felt at liberty to hear, judge, and determine for themselves, and to act in accordance with what the Bible, as they understood it, demanded of them." The congregants of South Butler resisted the worst excesses of antebellum American materialistic consumption, Ward believed, and could, therefore, hear and react more clearly to the scriptural admonition: "There is neither Jew nor Greek, there is neither bond nor free, there is neither male nor female, for ye are all one in Christ Jesus." Bourgeois society tended to mold everything—including people—into expendable commodities, as illustrated by the racist objectification of African Americans. But rather than following the dictates of modern culture, Ward's white church folk decided on a justice-oriented course of action based on their freely chosen response to the guidance of God's Word.[3]

Twenty-first-century Christians pose similar questions about the consequences of their actions as a result of their participation in the global economic system. As a result of their questioning, many of them have resolved to "eat local" in order to encourage small producers, family farms, and sustainable agriculture. Some spend time researching the supply chain of the products they buy so as not to unwittingly patronize sweat shops in the developing world. They recycle scrupulously. And they may spend extra money on a new car so that they will leave a smaller carbon footprint.

In Roman Catholic circles, Pope Francis promulgated an "apostolic exhortation" in 2013 that intended to guide the early actions of his papacy. In the document, he criticized unfettered markets and the growing economic disparity between rich and poor. The pope spoke out because many of the world's most wealthy countries, including the United States, experienced historic levels of income inequality in the early twenty-first century, which he interpreted as evidence of the structural sins of the economy. Francis decried the "idolatry of money,"

3. Samuel Ringgold Ward, *Autobiography of a Fugitive Negro* (1855; repr., Chicago: Johnson Publishing, 1970), 61.

warning that it will lead to "a new tyranny." In contrast, he outlined a populist agenda for the church, prodding Catholics in developed nations to reach out to the disenfranchised. "I prefer a church which is bruised, hurting, and dirty" to a smug and comfortable church. Many of today's radical evangelicals would agree.

10

Whatever Happened
to Evangelicalism?

The currents described in this book are, of course, not the whole of evangelicalism. Extensive immigration producing various ethnic denominations occurred primarily in the post–Civil War period. Such church bodies followed their own dynamic and became subject to American influences late in the story traced here. Likewise, highly confessional churches in Lutheran and related traditions, though deeply influenced by American revivalism, show divergent patterns of development. And within major denominations, elements like the "Old School" or "Princeton Theology" within Presbyterianism (more about this later) set themselves firmly against the currents of revivalism and thus against the reforms that revivalism generated.

But these other traditions were not at the heart of American evangelical experience in quite the same way as the currents traced in this book. Some of the other traditions have, in fact, been somewhat suspect from the viewpoint of "hardcore" evangelicalism. The extent to which the movements described in this book lie behind the institutions of evangelicalism may be seen, for example, when the editors of

Christianity Today survey Christian colleges for responses to some topic of current discussion. A majority of such institutions will be rooted in churches and movements mentioned in this book.

What happened, then, to the reforming spirit of evangelicalism? The answer is complex and perhaps can never be completely explained. Sociological, theological, historical, and psychological causes must be taken into account. This chapter is only an attempt at a tentative explanation.

First is the difficulty of maintaining for a long period of time any movement with the intensity of, for example, the Oberlin commitment to the antislavery struggle. Those who have surveyed the dynamic of Christian social reform in America have noticed an ebb-and-flow pattern alternating between periods of creative vitality and periods of stability when gains are consolidated and institutionalized. To some extent these latter periods are also a reaction against reform and a return to other emphases of the Christian tradition. This pattern may be seen when the turbulent 1960s gave way to the more tranquil and inner-directed styles of the seventies. From this perspective the surprising fact is that Oberlin, for example, was able to sustain its antislavery impulse from the mid-1830s through the Civil War.

But sociological interpretations of the dynamics of new movements also provide clues to the decline of evangelical reform. The groups that we have surveyed were in large part products of revival and renewal efforts not unlike such earlier movements as Quakerism and Methodism. In some cases, these currents resulted in the formation of new sects; in others, they were contained within larger denominations as a leavening influence. Sociologists have described how such movements often turn to the poor and disinherited for support and in the process recover themes of "preaching the gospel to the poor." Such movements also make high ethical demands and require a rigorous dedication to an all-consuming mission.

Succeeding generations, however, find these concerns greatly diluted. A first generation gathers by conviction around highly motivating issues and devotes its resources to a narrowly defined set of goals. In the second generation, resource and attention are diverted to the education and nurture of children in the ways of the movement. This generation fails, however, to grasp the original vision with the same intensity and finds subtle ways to twist the movement's institutions to its own concerns. This process continues through several generations until in many cases the very opposite of what was originally intended is finally produced. This dynamic may be seen in the successive history of the movements described in this book.

Finney's revivalism also built strong barriers against the rest of the world—often with distinct behavioral patterns that set the "true believer" off from the rest of society. The revivalistic ethic of "no smoking, drinking, and dancing" functioned in part in this way, but children growing up under such restraints experience them primarily as factors alienating them from their peers and society. This experience produces an overwhelming desire to belong, to feel at home in the dominant culture. Where behavioral distinctions are not abandoned entirely, they are bent and twisted to permit what they were intended to prohibit. When they remain, they are usually only a faint echo of a whole dissenting value system now discarded in the rush to cultural accommodation.

A poignant example of this dynamic is the reaction of children to having mothers who were ministers. Many of my peers have mothers or grandmothers who were ministers, but this fact was hidden from friends as strange and abnormal. Only with the broader cultural shift of values on this question have they admitted that their mothers functioned in such roles.

Similar dynamics may be detected on the social and economic levels, especially if adherents to a movement are drawn from the lower economic classes—a natural result of hearing and obeying the biblical injunction to "preach the gospel to the poor." Discipline and a reordered lifestyle enable converts to rise in social class and economic level, a process culminating in a middle-class church like those against which the movement originally protested. This new church is subtly transformed into a bastion against those who would threaten its life, especially the lower classes that were once a source of vitality.

Sensitive leaders of such movements, often intuitively aware of this dynamic, have warned against the "dangers of riches" that undercut the original force of revival movements. John Wesley often commented on this problem. "Christianity, true scriptural Christianity, has a tendency, in the process of time, to undermine and destroy itself. For wherever true Christianity spreads, it must cause diligence and frugality, which, in the natural course of things, must beget riches! And riches naturally beget pride, love of the world, and every temper that is destructive of Christianity. . . . Wherever it generally prevails, it saps its own foundation."

But such general considerations ought not to obscure a number of unique factors that contributed to the decline of nineteenth-century evangelical social involvement. The Civil War itself seems to have had a major impact. Finney's pre–Civil War revivalism was to some extent a reflection of the general optimism of the era that was a part of the youth of the nation and related to the seemingly endless frontiers to conquer. To evangelicals of the 1830s and '40s it was inconceivable that good values should ever come into fundamental conflict with one another. Oberlinites, for example, were committed in early years to both the peace movement and the antislavery crusade. But when slavery proved to be more entrenched than expected and the struggle against it began to require violence, the Oberlinites had to choose between conflicting loyalties. In opting for the antislavery struggle, they discovered that the world was more complicated than they thought. The Civil War helped to puncture earlier utopian visions and in doing so contributed to the dissolution of the reform impulse.

The Civil War also resolved—at least on the surface—the most profoundly social of the reform issues that revivalism had supported. Left after the war were the temperance movement, the "purity crusade," the anti-Masonry campaign, and related issues. These concerns were more susceptible to translation into questions of personal morality detached from the larger social framework. As a result, one detects in the post–Civil War period a growing concern for personal purity, understood increasingly as "no smoking, no drinking, no dancing, and no gambling"—the elements that came to characterize the revivalistic ethic of later days.

But the post–Civil War era brought even profounder disappointments to the evangelical dream. The revivalistic and reform movements had supported the broader expectation of a "Christian America" characterized by the incorporation into the legal and cultural life of the new nation of such principles as temperance, antislavery, Sabbath observance, and so on. Contemporary evangelicalism has for the most part not given up this dream. The issues that really mobilize the opposition of, for example, the National Association of Evangelicals are efforts to delete references to God from the public life of the nation—Supreme Court decisions to outlaw official prayers in public schools or Madalyn Murray O'Hair's campaign to prevent astronauts from reading the Scriptures from space. Similarly, earlier generations of evangelicals were deeply committed to prohibition and "blue laws" that restricted commercial activity on the Christian Sabbath (Sunday). Evangelicalism is still trying to cope with the fact that the United States has become a modern, secular, pluralistic state.

The post–Civil War period first began to force these questions on evangelicalism. Waves of immigration brought not only German Lutherans not inclined to follow the temperance banner but also Roman Catholics and Jews who had no place (other than as objects of conversion) in this dream of a Christian (read "Protestant"!) America. Massive urbanization and industrialization brought problems too complex for the revivalist reform vision. At the same time, attacks from without were intensified by the rise of biblical criticism, the emergence of Darwinism with its critique of the traditional view of human origins, and the difficulty of reconciling early chapters of Genesis with the new geological discoveries. Evangelicalism began to turn more and more in on itself to nurse the tattered remnants of the great vision for American life that had once thrust it out in aggressive reform.

Correlated with these issues were significant theological developments that reflected this pessimism and gave it additional strength. The first, and probably more important, of these developments took place in the doctrine of eschatology, the teaching about the events of the end times. Pre–Civil War evangelical eschatology was largely *postmillennial*, expecting Christ to return in judgment *after* a millennial reign of one thousand years. Post–Civil War evangelical eschatology was dominated by a new doctrine of *premillennialism*. This view expected Christ to return *before* the millennium to take the saints out of this world in an event called the "rapture."

Finney's revivalism, as well as that of Jonathan Blanchard, the Wesleyan Methodists, and other evangelical reformers, was tied to postmillennialism. Reform activity was in part to prepare the way for the millennium, which was in turn a reflection of the vision of the "state of the perfect society" that drew evangelicals into reform. Deeply intertwined was the evangelical dream of a Christian America whose fullest manifestation would not be unlike the ushering in of the millennium.

But this vision collapsed after the Civil War and was replaced by an eschatology that looked for the return of Christ to rescue the "saints" *out of this world*. Premillennial teaching implied that the world was in such bad shape that it would only get worse until the return of Christ. Some even argued that efforts to ameliorate social conditions would merely postpone the "blessed hope" of Christ's return by delaying the process of degeneration. Premillennialism was articulated to the evangelical world through conferences for the study of biblical prophecy that began in the 1870s and had a cumulative effect in the following decades. One major evangelical leader after another announced his conversion to the new views. The postwar revivalism of evangelist D. L. Moody was, for example, closely tied to this new eschatology. By the 1920s Wheaton College, originally motivated by the postmillennial vision of Jonathan Blanchard, had written premillennial doctrines into a theological platform by which the college is today governed and to which the faculty is required to give annual subscription.

Implicit in these differing eschatological visions are widely divergent views of the way God effects the divine will in the world. The postmillennial teaching emphasizes the efficacy of God's grace and gradual progress under its influence. Pre–Civil War evangelicals, on the one hand, expected to live on this earth in the millennium and to enjoy the fruits of their labor. The premillennial vision, on the other hand, is more impressed with the power of sin and evil and the fact that this world will soon have to be abandoned for a heavenly abode.

Those conditioned to think that evangelical theological discussions are resolved exclusively by scriptural exegesis would be astonished to discover the extent to which resolution of these eschatological issues depended upon matters of taste and perceptions of the direction in which the world was moving. Much of the appeal in the argumentation was to empirical evidence. The postmillennialists, on the one hand, pointed to the progress of foreign mission and the spread of literacy to prove that the world was in fact getting better and better. Premillennialists, on the other hand, cited the rise of crime and social problems, often primarily in the cities, as evidence that the world was growing more evil. Apparently a great deal depended on reading these "signs of the times"!

This shift in eschatology had profound, and somewhat mixed, impact on the social involvement of evangelicals. On the one hand, the expectation of the imminent return of Christ freed many from building for the immediate future (social advancement, pension plans, etc.) to give themselves wholeheartedly to the inner cities and foreign mission fields. Resulting contact with poor and oppressed peoples often pushed these devoted souls into relief and other welfare work—and occasionally into reform.

On the other hand, more characteristic was the tendency to abandon long-range social amelioration for a massive effort to preach the gospel to as many as possible before the return of Christ. The vision was now one of rescue from a fallen world. Just as Jesus was expected momentarily on the clouds to rapture his saints, so the slum worker established missions to rescue sinners out of the world to be among those to meet the Lord in the air. Evangelical effort that had once provided the impulse and troops for reform rallies was rechanneled into exegetical speculation about the timing of Christ's return and into maintenance of the expanding prophecy conferences.

The extent to which this shift in eschatology was felt throughout evangelical life and thought is difficult to overestimate. One of the most striking contrasts between pre–Civil War revivalists and those after the war is that the former founded liberal arts colleges while the latter established Bible schools. To the postwar premillennialist the liberal arts college involved too much affirmation of the cultural values of this world and took time away from the crucial task of getting a minimal knowledge of the Bible before rushing into the inner cities or the mission fields to gather as many souls as possible before the imminent return of Christ. In the late nineteenth century the Bible school movement picked up the message of the prophecy conferences and trained a whole generation of evangelicals in the new doctrines. (One sign of how little premillennial eschatology really influences the practice of contemporary evangelicals—in spite of the popularity of Hal Lindsey's best-selling interpretations of it—is seen in the fact that over the last generation many of these Bible schools have been gradually transformed into liberal arts colleges!)

But in addition to the rise of premillennialism, another major theological shift in evangelicalism undercut the social reform of earlier years: the growth in impact among evangelicals of the "Old School" of Presbyterianism, especially as it found expression in the "Princeton Theology." This theology is so called because it held sway at Princeton Theological Seminary from its founding in 1812 until the twentieth-century split that produced Westminster Theological Seminary. The Princeton Theology was grounded in Protestant scholasticism and represented the major articulation of the "Old Calvinism" against which Finney and his followers had reacted so strongly. The Princeton theologians, on their side, were horrified with both Finney's theology and his social views—as well as revivalism in general.

In the nineteenth century Finney's "New School" Presbyterian views dominated evangelicalism, while the twentieth century saw the increasing impact of the Old School Princeton Theology. This shift is widely discernible in evangelicalism in the most surprising places. A striking example of this reversal may be seen in the history of Gordon College and Gordon-Conwell Theological Seminary, today the dominant evangelical schools in New England. These schools are rooted in the work of A. J. Gordon, whose abolitionism and feminism we have already discussed. Though Baptist, Gordon stood very much in tradition of Finney and, as such, was often the object of the sharp polemics of Benjamin B. Warfield, the major exponent of the Princeton Theology at the turn of the twentieth century. Yet more recently Gordon-Conwell has become one of the major advocacy centers of the Princeton Theology mediated through Westminster Theological Seminary. Similar shifts occurred at Congregationalist Wheaton College, and by the 1950s even the Wesleyan Methodists were advocating certain formulations of the Princeton Theology.

The significance of such developments for evangelical social reform is that the Princeton Theology incarnated extremely conservative social views. Charles Hodge, the major figure of this school said at the semi-centennial celebration of his work at Princeton, "I am not afraid to say that a new idea never originated in this seminary." Though intended to speak of theology, this comment also indicates the conservative temperament of Hodge in other areas. He explicitly affirmed that the church should be a conservative force in society. Of the Presbyterian Church he commented in 1861 that "we have preserved the integrity and unity of the Church, made it the great conservative body of truth, moderation, and liberty of conscience in our country."

This position pitted Hodge and the Princeton school firmly against Finney and the abolitionists. Hodge was disturbed by the abolitionist attack on so basic a structure of American society as slavery, insisting that Christianity was never "designed to tear up the institutions of society by its roots." In an attack on those like Finney who urged civil disobedience of the Fugitive Slave Laws, he argued that the abolitionists were "a small minority of the people. They have never included in their ranks either the controlling intellect or moral feeling at the North. Their fundamental principle is anti-scriptural and therefore irreligious. They assume that slaveholding is sinful. This doctrine is the life of the sect. It has no power over those who reject that principle, and therefore it has not gained ascendancy over those whose faith is governed by the word of God." Hodge concluded that "both political despotism and domestic slavery, belong in morals to the *adiaphora*, to things indifferent."

Hodge did insist that slaveholders follow certain biblical norms that would moderate the extremes of slavery. He also hinted that over a long period of time education and moral training of slaves might so elevate them that emancipation would be appropriate. And when emancipation did come, he supported it. But it is important to notice how Hodge's position functioned in the antislavery struggle. His writings were used not only against the abolitionists but also to defend slavery as such. They appeared, for example, in *Cotton Is King, and Pro-Slavery Arguments*, a major Southern defense of American slavery.

Hodge and the Princeton school also opposed the women's movement that emerged from abolitionism. Hodge argued that "females and minors are judged (though for different reasons), incompetent to the proper discharge of the duties of citizenship." For Hodge there was "no form of human excellence before which we bow with profounder deference than that which appears in a delicate woman adorned with the inward graces, and devoted to the peculiar duties of her sex; and there is no deformity of human character from which we turn with deeper loathing than from a woman forgetful of her nature and clamorous for the vocations and rights of men." Princeton theologians therefore opposed suffrage, arguing that the idea of two autonomous votes in a single household was irreconcilable with the biblical doctrine of the headship of the husband.

The contrast between the social positions of Finney and Hodge has to be understood on several levels. There are hints of social conditioning. Though Hodge opposed some of the church structures that contributed to the situation, the Princeton Theology was more closely tied to the aristocracy and higher social classes. While Finney was willing to cultivate these classes and was proud of his success among them, his revivalism and his social commitments drew him more to identification with the poor, the slave, and the masses—at least to some extent. Both Hodge and Finney, therefore, represented to a certain extent in their thought the interests of those with whom they had aligned themselves sociologically.

But such analysis is not adequate by itself and cannot explain, for example, the Tappan brothers. There were also fundamental differences in theology that can be correlated with the divergent social positions. The Princeton Theology was a highly intellectualized tradition that understood faith in a largely doctrinal sense and placed a high premium on orthodoxy and "right doctrine." While Oberlin was not anti-intellectual and produced its own theology, it was more oriented to questions of ethics, action, and "right doing" or "right being."

Finney and Hodge also took significantly different positions on the question of determinism. Finney detested the determinism of "Old School Calvinism" and regularly denounced it. In affirming determinism, Hodge tended to argue that everything is done according to God's good purposes, and that whatever our position in life, we ought not to resist it, but find what good God wishes to work in that situation. In this view poverty becomes not only an unfortunate situation out of which God is able to bring good, but even more a result of a direct determination of God not to be resisted. Such a position not only supports the status quo but also gives to it a divine endorsement.

But probably the most important theological distinction between Finney and Hodge was the relative emphasis they gave to sin and redemption. The Princeton theologians were deeply impressed by the presence of sin in the world. Hodge, for example, maintained that one implication of human depravity is that "no man, no community of men, no society, church or nation ever suffered in this life as much as their sins deserve. And, consequently, no individual or nation can ever justly complain of the dispensation of Divine providence as unmerited inflictions." The Princeton theologians also firmly resisted the idea of God's grace overcoming sin in this life. In doing this they came perilously close to making the sinful state a normative one.

Finney, however, placed greater weight on redemption and the power of God's grace to transform sinful persons and society. The significance of this shift is especially clear in discussions of the women's issue. Princeton theologians, deeply conscious of the impact of sin, tended, on the one hand, to focus on the curse in the Genesis narrative of the fall, arguing that the subordination of women in that passage provided a universal principle normative for all human life this side of the grave. Finney and the Oberlinites tended, on the other hand, to see the curse as descriptive of the sinful state out of which redemption is to be effected. In this perspective women may be elevated, especially in the church, to a position of equality.

In other words, Finney's emphasis on redemption provided that utopian edge necessary for a theology to support major social change. The importance of this theologically grounded utopianism has again become clear in discussions between the South American theologies of liberation and the school of Christian realism that dominated much mid- to late-twentieth-century American theology. Christian realists find the liberation theologians' use of utopianism visionary and unrealistic. The Latin American theologians reply that without this theme the positions of the Christian realists become in effect "ideologies of the establishment."[1] By analogy, Hodge was in his time a very conservative "Christian realist" whose theology served as an "ideology of the establishment." Though accused of perfectionism by the Princeton theologians, Finney and his followers found in the doctrine of redemption the utopian vision that enabled them to press toward a society free of slavery and the subordination of women.

These theological insights also help us to understand how the Princeton Theology gained ascendancy in the evangelical world. It incarnated the same tendency toward pessimism that was in premillennialism. Ernest Sandeen has argued in his *Roots of Fundamentalism* that the "biblical literalism" underlying both the prophecy conference movement and Princeton Theology doctrinalism formed the bridge by which the two movements were able to coalesce in the late nineteenth century into a mixture that laid the basis for modern fundamentalism.[2] What is suggested here is that a common tendency toward a pessimistic worldview was another bridge that permitted this coalescing.

If there is any validity to the analysis of the differing social contexts that lay behind the Princeton and Oberlin theologies, that analysis suggests that as the movements and denominations formed in response to nineteenth-century revivalism and rose socially and economically, they found the Princeton views more congenial to their new social positions. As they climbed higher in the social structure and became more and more a part of the established order, the Princeton Theology would have been more attractive precisely because it could function as an "ideology of the establishment."

And again, sociologists have described how movements that concentrate on ethics and religious experience in the first generation often shift to doctrine in succeeding generations. This movement from "being" and "doing" to "believing" could also support a new openness to the emphases of the Princeton theologians. Whatever

1. For an overview of this discussion, see the foreword by William Lazareth to José Miguez Bonino, *Doing Theology in a Revolutionary Situation* (Philadelphia: Fortress Press, 1975).

2. Ernest R. Sandeen, *The Roots of Fundamentalism: British and American Millenarianism, 1800–1930* (Chicago: University of Chicago Press, 1970).

the precise cause, it is clear that one can trace in evangelicalism a growing emphasis on "right doctrine" (orthodoxy) as the measure of acceptability and a consequent shift away from religious experience (orthopathy) and behavioral norms (orthopraxy).

A final possible reason for the twentieth-century ascendancy of the Princeton Theology in evangelicalism may be the rise of biblical criticism. The Princeton theologians had early on marshaled their forces to build a doctrine of "biblical inerrancy" adequate to resist the rising tides of criticism. Other traditions less well prepared for this struggle reached for the Princeton formulations and in the process incorporated other theological and social perspectives of the school.

But whatever the precise reasons for the rise of the Princeton Theology and its coalescing with the new premillennial doctrines, in this process we see both the rise of fundamentalism and the decline of evangelical social involvement. This development is summarized by Otto Piper of a later day at Princeton in discussing the contributions of various nations to the development of Christian ethics. He suggests that

> characteristic of American church life is a succession of nationwide ethical campaigns, in which the interest is focused on the abolition of some single evil, for instance the emancipation of the slaves, prohibition of alcoholic beverages, pacifism, or, civil rights for African Americans. A contribution of lasting significance was made by Finney's (1792–1875) insistence on holiness. He did not only denounce the depravity of the sinner, as was common in the revival movements, but also pointed out the blessings of the Spirit's sanctifying power, by which a person's conduct is radically transformed. In turn, the one-sided predilection which dispensationalism and fundamentalism showed for theological correctness was not conducive to the development of ethical responsibility.[3]

In the fundamentalist/modernist controversy and in succeeding decades, the sociological, theological, and historical currents produced a movement that in many ways stood for the opposite of what an earlier generation of evangelicals had affirmed. What had begun as

3. Otto Piper, *Christian Ethics* (London: Thomas Nelson, 1970), 21.

a Christian egalitarianism was transformed into a type of Christian elitism. Revivalistic currents that had once been bent to the liberation of the slave now allied themselves with wealth and power against the civil rights movement. Churches and movements that had pioneered a new role for women became the most resistant to contemporary movements seeking the same goals.

In the process the rewriting of history began to take place. Early- to mid-twentieth-century evangelical editors of Finney's writings proceeded to edit out references to social reform. When a 1900 biography of evangelist Dwight L. Moody was reissued in 1930, some significant alterations had been made. The first edition reported that in the Civil War Moody "could not conscientiously enlist" because "there has never been a time in my life when I felt I could take a gun and shoot down a fellow being. In this respect I am a Quaker." But the later edition, published at a time in which pacifism was farther from evangelical thinking, reports that Moody refused to serve because he had "dedicated himself to Christian service"—implying that a "higher calling" rather than conscientious scruples was his reason.[4] In 1943 the Wesleyan Methodists celebrated the one hundredth anniversary of their founding with a special issue of the *Wesleyan Methodist*. But one has to search diligently for any reference to the slavery issue that brought the movement into existence. The reader is left with the impression that a group of highly spiritual men spontaneously came together to found a new denomination to lift up anew the spiritual message of the Wesleyan Revival as the fullest expression of New Testament truth.

Thus a great heritage of evangelical social witness was buried and largely forgotten, and the stage was set for the ironic struggles of the 1960s in which the spiritual descendants of earlier evangelical social activists would reject the modern manifestations of the reform impulse as inherently unbiblical and opposed to the spirit of evangelical Christianity.

---

4. These alterations are detected by Guy Franklin Hershberger, *The Way of the Cross in Human Relations* (Scottdale, PA: Herald Press, 1958), chap. 8.

Epilogue to the
First Edition (1976)

Reflections on Some Unresolved Issues

By Donald W. Dayton

This study leaves many unresolved issues, most beyond the scope of this book. Questions of eschatology or the choice of competing theological systems cannot be resolved by history or by the extent to which such positions contribute to, or undermine, Christian social witness, though such considerations would surely play a part in the process. Nor can the evangelical heritage here discovered be appropriated directly for our age without careful rethinking of important exegetical and theological questions or without careful analysis of the differences between the nineteenth and twentieth centuries. But the material surveyed in this book not only helps one to understand contemporary evangelicalism but also calls into question some of the basic categories by which it is usually interpreted.

The history related in this book has, for example, forced me even to understand the word "evangelical" in new ways. Today this label generally derives its connotations from the fundamentalist/modernist controversy of the early decades of this century. In the 1940s a second generation of fundamentalists called themselves "evangelicals" in part to project a more positive image. When used by this "post-fundamentalist" party, the word is understood largely in terms of paradigms like the struggle within Presbyterianism that climaxed in the founding of Westminster Theological Seminary, an effort to preserve intact the Princeton Theology of the nineteenth century. According to this understanding the fundamentalist or evangelical is one who holds true to orthodox Christian faith (usually very narrowly defined) over against those who have diluted it by the acceptance of biblical criticism, evolution, the social gospel, and other modern liberal currents.

With the intellectual ascendency within contemporary evangelicalism of the "post-fundamentalist" party, the whole has come more and more to be understood in terms of this analysis. This perspective is clearly apparent, for example, in a 1975 interpretation titled *The Evangelicals*. In an introductory essay delineating the "Theological Boundaries of Evangelical Faith," church historian John Gerstner equates evangelicalism with the "Princeton school which had come to be recognized as the nineteenth-century standard-bearer of evangelical orthodoxy." Clearly reflecting the nineteenth-century antipathy between Oberlin and Princeton (as indicated in the last chapter), Gerstner then finds that "Finney, the greatest of nineteenth-century evangelists, became the greatest of nineteenth-century foes of evangelicalism."[1]

The rise of this perspective has not only contributed to the decline of evangelical social witness, as indicated in the preceding chapter, but has also tended to distort evangelical historiography. Much more of modern evangelicalism would stand, historically at least, in the succession of Finney and Oberlin than Hodge and Princeton. And when American church historians use the term "evangelical," they generally refer to the emergence of the Arminian, pietistic revivalism that was epitomized in Finney and marked the end of the cultural dominance of the "Old Calvinism" preserved in the Princeton Theology and many modern post-fundamentalist evangelicals. Ironically this nineteenth-century evangelicalism was highly motivated by

1. David F. Wells and John D. Woodbridge, eds., *The Evangelicals: What They Believe, Who They Are, Where They Are Changing* (Nashville: Abingdon, 1975), 28–29.

a self-conscious repudiation of what has come to be the dominant theological system in modern evangelicalism.

The importance of distinguishing these two types of evangelicalism can be seen on several levels.[2] In spite of a great deal of overlap, the two types focus on different areas of major concern. We have seen some of this in the contrasts between Oberlin and Princeton in the last chapter. The modern type of evangelicalism, on the one hand, with its roots in Princeton places a premium on "right doctrine" and the preservation of a particular brand of "orthodoxy." Eighteenth- and nineteenth-century evangelicalism, on the other hand, was more concerned with the personal appropriation of grace—with conversion and the "new life" that follows the "new birth." These evangelicals, though not unorthodox in a broader sense, emphasized that Christian faith that lacks vitality or is "unrevived" comes in several varieties, including orthodox. John Wesley, for example, never tired of affirming that "neither does religion consist in orthodoxy or right opinions. . . . A man may be orthodox in every point. . . . He may be almost as orthodox as the Devil . . . and may, all the while, be as great a stranger as he to the religion of the heart."

This contrast can, of course, be overdrawn. The earlier evangelicals were not without a concern for the preservation of genuine Christianity, and modern evangelicals certainly stress Christian experience. But differing accents had profound social consequences. It was revivalist evangelicalism that supported the antislavery movement and opened up new roles for women. Even modern post-fundamentalist evangelicals usually point to the Evangelical Revival in England or to pre–Civil War revivalism as the prime examples of evangelical social involvement, though generally without showing awareness of the differences between revivalism and fundamentalism.

But rejection of the modern fundamentalist paradigm of evangelicalism has also required another shift in categories of analysis.

2. For a helpful confirmation of this distinction see the sharp polemic against the label "conservative Evangelical" by Presbyterian Ralph Winter of Fuller Theological Seminary in the introduction to his anthology, *The Evangelical Response to Bangkok* (South Pasadena, CA: William Carey Library, 1973). Winter understands evangelicalism primarily in terms of the nineteenth-century type I am describing here.

As illustrated in the preceding chapter, full understanding of revival-istic evangelicalism has required the incorporation of historical and sociological categories into the theological analysis usually offered by adherents of modern evangelicalism. The revivalist movement incarnated an element of protest against nominal Christianity and the traditional churches that sometimes manifested itself in a rather sectarian dynamic. If one is to judge by either the membership of the National Association of Evangelicals or by the movements that lie behind the colleges and seminaries recommended in the pages of *Christianity Today*, much of contemporary evangelicalism is rooted in the various sects, renewal movements, and new denominations spawned in the wake of nineteenth-century revivalism.

These currents require sociological categories for full interpreta-tion. It is possible to detect in such movements a certain centrifugal movement in which these protest and revival forces spin out from the patterns of traditional church life (hierarchical structures, liturgical worship, a trained clergy class, broad cultural affirmation, and so forth) to a more egalitarian, spontaneous, lay-oriented, and narrowly focused style of church life. The result is often a highly innovative, but culturally marginal, movement identified with the disenfranchised of society. But this centrifugal movement is usually followed by a corresponding but opposite centripetal movement back toward the center and affirmation of more traditional forms of church life, trained clergy, more elaborate worship, establishment values, and so forth.

Once discerned this dynamic greatly illumines the ironies of the history sketched in this book. Movements whose egalitarian thrust once manifested itself in feminism and abolitionism had by the mid-twentieth century moved back toward more traditional patterns of church life and social views. One reason for the intense clash of the evangelical world with the rise of the social movements of the 1960s was that the post–World War II generation of evangelicals was at the height of its centripetal thrust. Evangelicalism was moving toward the center just as secularized, centrifugal, countercultural movements were spinning off in the opposite direction.

This centrifugal/centripetal dynamic also helps to explain a surpris-ing number of phenomena in the contemporary evangelical world.

The amazing growth of evangelical theological seminaries in the mid-twentieth century has been much analyzed in the religious press, and a variety of possible reasons have been advanced. What has not been noticed is that the evangelical seminaries were vigorous and expanding because they were in many cases a century younger than the more established seminaries and were rooted largely in the post–World War II evangelical rediscovery of theological education and the values of a trained clergy. Bethel Theological Seminary and Trinity Evangelical Divinity School are supported by small ethnic churches produced by nineteenth-century revivalist and free church currents. Asbury Theological Seminary represents not so much the "orthodox" party within Methodism as the nineteenth-century Holiness movement that emerged from revivalist sources. Gordon-Conwell is probably best understood as the product of similar phenomena within Baptist contexts. Even interdenominational Fuller Theological Seminary in California fits the patterns of the other seminaries in terms of growth patterns and post–World War II founding.

This same centrifugal/centripetal dynamic also helps explain some of the tensions surfacing among those persons calling for a renewal of evangelical social concern. For some this is a further step in moving toward the center. These persons call for a "responsible" social witness grounded in broader cultural affirmation correlatable with upward social mobility. But it is also possible to discern among other evangelicals a renewal of the centrifugal thrust in protest against, and repudiation of, an evangelicalism that has become bourgeois and establishment oriented. One often finds among these persons themes of restoration and renewal (and even occasionally a call for restoration of the "New Testament church"), a tendency toward communitarian and other countercultural lifestyles, a willingness to draw on the charismatic renewal movements, frequent withdrawal from traditional churches to found house church movements, and so forth. This protest against the bourgeois church has many similarities to patterns of nineteenth-century sectarianism.

These conflicting thrusts are often intermingled within the same groups and even within individuals. But evidence of a certain sorting-out process continues to accumulate, and soon we may be able to discern whether the calls for a renewal of evangelical social witness are the final steps in the "maturation" (or "decline," depending on one's perspective) of evangelicalism, or perhaps the first steps of new protest movements not unlike those of the nineteenth century, though no doubt given different shape and character by the new contexts of today.

Conclusion to the Second Edition (2014)

A Trajectory of Integrated Faith

By Douglas M. Strong

When first published in the mid-1970s, the vignettes of nine-teenth-century figures, movements, and events that Donald Dayton recounted in *Discovering an Evangelical Heritage* helped to shape the self-perceptions and inform the vocational directions of many Christians. Dayton provided a historical grounding for an inspiring narrative of American Christianity that stressed the biblically based integration of revivalism with social-reform activism. When up-and-coming evangelical leaders such as Jim Wallis, Ronald Sider, John Perkins, and Tony Campolo became aware of this holistic legacy, they felt emboldened by the example of the past to advocate for a faith-based, justice-oriented praxis as the best agenda and trajectory for evangelicalism's future. An activist, conversion-centered expression of faith, similar to what was promulgated by the 1973 Chicago Declaration of Evangelical Social Concern, appeared to be the most relevant and forward-looking religious option of late-twentieth-century Christianity—and a growing one at that. Those were heady days, when a revived evangelicalism seemed poised to generate a significant influence on the religious culture of the United States.

Post-1980 Transitions within Evangelicalism

The renewal of evangelical social engagement flourished in the post-1960s milieu. But the relatively high profile of 1970s social-justice evangelicalism was eclipsed in the 1980s by the impact of televangelists Jerry Falwell, Pat Robertson, and Jim Bakker, who drew the spotlight of the media by their sometimes inflammatory religious rhetoric. These conservative preachers reviled the popular justice-oriented evangelicalism of their time as an aberration from doctrinal orthodoxy and as a dangerous melding of religious conviction with "left-wing" proposals. Meanwhile, most religious and political liberals also disdained the new crop of evangelicals; they perceived "radical evangelicalism" (to use Jim Wallis's term) as an incongruent self-contradiction.

Conservative challenges to the Chicago Declaration–variety of evangelicalism began with the rise of the Moral Majority, founded by Falwell in 1979. Issues related to personal morality, such as abortion and homosexuality, and issues related to the role of Christianity in the public square, such as school prayer, dominated the social and political agenda of the Moral Majority. Prior to about 1980, Falwell and the other televangelists had been viewed, and described themselves, as "fundamentalists," but now they started to refer to themselves as "evangelicals." By appropriating the evangelical mantle, the former fundamentalists effectively pushed the entire neo-evangelical movement toward the right, at least in the public's perception. This move also had the effect of causing more socially conscious (but still pietistic) Christians to shy away from referring to themselves as evangelicals. Some wanted to abandon the word and leave it to the conservatives (or, later, added qualifiers, describing themselves as "progressive evangelicals" or "post-evangelicals"). Others migrated toward liberal Protestantism. By 1991, even Donald Dayton wondered about the term's usefulness.[1] A sharp contrast developed between various religious positions. Fervent Christian faith came to be identified with political conservatism, while political liberalism began to be associated with secularism. Sociologically, the post-1980 period has been recognized as a time when "culture wars" defined and divided Americans, both religiously and sociopolitically.[2]

During the 1970s, evangelicalism was frequently described as a big-tent movement centered on experiential piety and witness to Christ through word and deed. This broad evangelical perspective took its cues from the eighteenth-century preaching of Whitefield, Edwards, and Wesley and from the nineteenth-century revivalistic reform represented by Finney and his followers. Such an affective, practically oriented, born-again ethos made room for a number of options, both political (conservative, moderate, progressive) and theological (Arminian, Calvinist, Anabaptist, charismatic, etc.). By the 1980s and beyond, however, the popular understanding of the evangelical label became less fluid. The bandwidth of the movement returned to the neo-evangelical, post-fundamentalist boundaries characteristic of the 1950s and 1960s, and sometimes even veered back toward the narrowness of 1920s fundamentalism. Late-twentieth-century evangelicalism came to be identified only with political conservatism and/or doctrinal propositionalism.

Evangelical church membership nonetheless continued to grow in the 1980s and 1990s. Megachurches proliferated, led by noted preachers such as Bill Hybels, Rick Warren, T. D. Jakes, and Charles Stanley. Evangelicals increased their political and cultural influence, counting presidents Ronald Reagan and George W. Bush among their number, along with many other politicians and businesspeople. By 2012, neo-evangelical leaders, including the president of the National Association of Evangelicals (NAE), saw themselves as "emerging from the margins," since they were "now at the center of power."[3] But while

1. Donald W. Dayton, "Some Doubts about the Usefulness of the Category 'Evangelical,'" in *The Variety of American Evangelicalism* (Knoxville: University of Tennessee Press, 1991), 245–55.

2. James Davison Hunter, *Culture Wars: The Struggle to Define America* (New York: Basic Books, 1991).

3. Leith Anderson, panel presentation at the Association of Theological Schools meeting, Minneapolis, MN, June 21, 2012.

growing, evangelicalism was a less diverse movement—in terms of its theological and political breadth—than it had been in the 1970s.

This constriction became evident initially in 1980. The election campaign that year signified a turn to the right, when many conservative Christians expressed their contempt for Jimmy Carter's social policies, even though he insisted that they were faith-based. They also repudiated Carter's accent on a restrained foreign policy and international negotiations. In contrast to Carter's call for limits on US ambition, the "New Religious Right" desired a return to an emphasis on national triumphalism. This stress on American exceptionalism grew to such an extent that some Christians during the 1980 campaign insisted that retaining the Panama Canal as an American territory was an important litmus test of religious (and not just political) purity. Somewhat paradoxically, at the same time that this patriotic jingoism prevailed, many conservative Christians also embraced the pessimistic premillennialism characteristic of authors such as Hal Lindsey, who declared that the "late, great planet Earth" was on its way to hell. Why care for society, they asked, when God will snatch ("rapture") us from this doomed globe and take us away to heaven?

Another significant pushback regarding the new directions taken by 1970s evangelicalism came from conservatives' objections to Chicago Declaration–type initiatives that challenged American racism. In the early 1980s, political activist Lee Atwater developed a "Southern strategy" of using racial wedge issues to win over white voters. Atwater subtly linked the religious identification of the Southern electorate to their fears regarding what was happening to the dominant culture.[4] He thereby succeeded in constructing a correlation between evangelicalism and the political right, at least in the depictions made by most news outlets—a perception that has continued today. In a typical 2012 *New York Times* article, for example, evangelicals were not represented by a theological description, but by a cultural description as "Christians on the right." The article also claimed, vice

4. N. A. Valentino and D. O. Sears, "Race and Partisan Realignment in the Contemporary South," *American Journal of Political Science* 49, no. 3 (July 2005): 672–88.

versa, that "evangelical Christians" are the "one bedrock element of the conservative movement."[5]

While the press tended to view post-1980 evangelicals primarily in terms of their sociopolitical positions, there was also a tightening of theological positions during this period. For many religious conservatives, the term "evangelical" became synonymous with a type of Reformed scholasticism and biblical literalism. Neo-Calvinists John Piper, Wayne Grudem, and some leaders of the Southern Baptist Convention (such as Albert Mohler and others who asserted that Calvinism was the only appropriate theological framework for Baptists) promulgated this perspective as the "received evangelical tradition." The theology they articulated was expressed through the lens of modern categories of propositional truth. According to theologian Roger Olson, such evangelical leaders "perceive an identity crisis within evangelicalism" and "tend to regard right doctrine as the *sine qua non* of evangelical identity; for them . . . evangelicalism is primarily a mental category—defined by firm cognitive boundaries."[6]

In the nineteenth century, the predominant exemplars of evangelicalism were Methodists, Arminianized Baptists, and New School Presbyterians and Congregationalists, all of whom spoke and wrote about the new birth in Christ and holiness through the agency of the Spirit. Certain affections ("orthopathy," or commonly held experiences of faith) and ethical behaviors ("orthopraxy," or commonly held commitments to charity and justice) thus characterized nineteenth-century evangelicalism. (These emphases also prevailed among many evangelicals in the 1970s, such as Dayton, Wallis, and Sider.) But the primary default understanding of evangelicalism for much of the twentieth century and into the early twenty-first century has been an affirmation of specific doctrines ("orthodoxy," or commonly held beliefs), including a strict interpretation of biblical inerrancy. In that vein, it is revealing that Leith Anderson declared in 2012 that, in his opinion as the leader of the NAE, the only common trait of evangelicals is

5. "Christians on the Right Urge Reform on Migrants," *New York Times*, June 13, 2012, A16.

6. Roger Olson, http://relevancy22. blogspot.com/2013/03/roger-olson-history -of-evangelicalism21.html.

a particular understanding of the source of authority for Christian belief and practice. He maintained that the one distinguishing element of evangelicals is that they all hold that "the church is the product of the Bible and not the Bible a product of the church"[7]—in effect, a sixteenth- and seventeenth-century magisterial Reformation-era definition, not the eighteenth- and nineteenth-century free-church/pietistic definition of evangelicalism (such as that written about by Robert Baird) in which a revivalistic, regenerative experience was viewed as the determinative factor.

What makes one an "evangelical," theologically? Differing answers have been given to this question. One answer has been provided by the post-fundamentalist Evangelical Theological Society (ETS), which disallowed any variance of perspective, so much so that the society almost stripped biblical scholar Robert Gundry and theologian Clark Pinnock of their memberships, due to their respective articulations of a broad view of scriptural authority and an Arminian-influenced "open theism." For the ETS, neo-Calvinist inerrancy was conveyed as the sole representative voice of evangelicalism. Some young Christians are attracted to the perceived clarity and definitiveness of such a dogmatic stance, as seen by the popularity of congregations like Bethlehem Baptist Church in Minneapolis and Mars Hill Church in Seattle, where—for example—traditional gender roles are taught to young people according to a "complementarian" (and allegedly literal) interpretation of New Testament texts about women, in contrast to an egalitarian interpretation.

A New Generation Searching for an Integrated Christianity

But an even greater number of younger evangelicals in the twenty-first century—like their antecedents in the 1840s and the 1970s—are more interested in Spirit-led piety than in doctrinal purity. They are seeking an integration of their commitment to Christ with their social activism. Social concern interests are flowering as they did after the 1960s. Millennials are passionate regarding God and compassionate

---

7. Anderson, panel presentation at the Association of Theological Schools meeting.

regarding the needs of the world. They demand a focus on Jesus *and* justice—a holistic biblical faith.[8] They are impatient with the divisiveness and culture-bashing that they see manifest in the churches of their parents. Young adult evangelicals, according to Mark Tauber, the publisher of HarperOne, are either "having trouble understanding why the traditional lines make sense and/or [are] just outright rejecting those lines." In 2012, CNN's Belief Blog asked religious leaders how faith is shaping the world. Cameron Strang, publisher of *Relevant* magazine, stated that "the worldview of most younger Christians already differs from previous generations regarding social justice, cultural engagement and politics." Samuel Rodriguez, the president of the National Hispanic Christian Leadership Conference, foresees that "America's born-again community will have an opportunity to contextualize an alternative narrative to the polarizing elements from both the right and the left by reconciling the righteousness message of Billy Graham with the justice platform of Dr. Martin Luther King, Jr." Harry R. Jackson Jr., the pastor of the multicultural Hope Christian Church in suburban Washington, DC, predicts that the future of Christianity will exhibit "political and social engagement by a younger/more racially diverse, evangelical people."[9]

These young, diverse evangelicals are troubled by racial injustice, a still largely untreated, often unacknowledged, and lingering sin of American society. But other issues engage them too. They recognize that women continue to suffer from gender inequality, particularly regarding leadership roles in the conservative congregations from which many Christian college students hail. They encounter friends who are in same-sex relationships, and so they find themselves entering into ethical currents difficult for them to navigate. Matters of sustainability and ecological degradation motivate them, which they read about in the writings of Wendell Berry and which they promote through the Evangelical Environmental Network. Poverty and violence

8. "How Technology Is Changing Millennial Faith," *Barna: Millennials*, October 15, 2013, https://www.barna.org/barna-update/millennials/640-how-technology-is-changing-millennial-faith.

9. "15 Faith-Based Predictions for 2012," *CNN Belief Blog*, January 1, 2012, http://religion.blogs.cnn.com/2012/01/01/12-faith-based-predictions-for-2012/.

in American society disturb them and cause them to speak out for change. The (New) Abolitionist Movement compels students today like it did in the 1830s with students from Lane Theological Seminary and Oberlin College. The agitation to end modern-day slavery has galvanized undergraduate enthusiasm at Christian colleges; groups like International Justice Mission and Not for Sale assist them with their involvement. They also start their own ministry organizations.

Young-adult evangelicals are seeking precursors for their work in the struggles against human trafficking, racial injustice, and other pressing problems. They find themselves drawn to some of the non-profits developed decades ago, such as the Sojourners community, Evangelicals for Social Action, World Vision, World Relief, the Lausanne Committee, the World Evangelical Fellowship, Christians for Biblical Equality, and countless local urban and rural ministries. They look back, as well, to examples from the nineteenth century.

Fresh understandings and explorations about the nature of the church also interest young Christians, similar to the large number of ecclesial schemes that evolved in the 1970s, and representing the sectarian, centrifugal forces that Dayton wrote about in the preceding chapter. They are intrigued by communal church experiments and intentional living communities, including the new monasticism personified by Shane Claiborne. They talk about the church as both "ancient" and simultaneously "future." Christians today want to know the history of their theological forebears and to pay attention to what the church universal has thought about belief and practice. Some see an affinity with the liturgical innovation and "generous orthodoxy" of the Emerging Church movement of Brian McLaren, Tony Jones, and Rob Bell—though others perceive these Emergent teachings as going beyond classic evangelicalism.

Christian college students are more active than ever. Social venture projects excite them, and they are inspired by World Vision's Richard Stearns (*The Hole in Our Gospel*) and Hope International's Peter Greer (*The Poor Will Be Glad*). While preaching to undergraduates at Seattle Pacific University in 2012, the eighty-one-year-old John Perkins boldly stated that "this is a wonderful day" because "this is the greatest generation of the evangelical church." Perkins was convinced that millennial Christians are the greatest generation because they value higher education, they understand the importance of economic justice, and they want a "holistic redemption" that includes a mandate for renewing the environment and other social reconstructive efforts.[10]

Where an earlier generation might have undertaken evangelistic missions, this generation—while not neglecting the verbal proclamation of the gospel—wants their proclamation to occur through activism, such as teaching in the inner city, starting microfinance initiatives to end global poverty, or changing the world through creative entrepreneurship via new technologies. So what is the role of evangelism in such scenarios? The older, neo-evangelical outlook would state that "social justice is a value but evangelism is a higher value than social justice."[11] Younger evangelicals insist on emphasizing both concurrently. They want to stress love for God and love for God's world. Soong-Chan Rah, for instance, writes about how immigrant evangelical churches offer a model in which "evangelism is the engagement of life on all levels—serving a community in need and providing the services that demonstrate the kingdom of God to those who may be experiencing a displacement in the kingdom of this world."[12]

Most millennial Christians are searching for a faith that is connected to the Jesus of the Bible and applicable to the problems of today. According to David Kinnaman, "They are not disillusioned with tradition; they are frustrated with slick or shallow expressions of religion."[13] They want a history and a theology big enough to support their praxis. For these emerging adults, there remains an "evangelical heritage" to be rediscovered. Just as the story of nineteenth-century socially conscious Christian believers touched a nerve with 1970s radical evangelicals who were looking for a usable past to assist them in their social justice activities, Christian college students and many others in

10. John Perkins, "The Seventh Annual John Perkins Lecture," Seattle Pacific University, Seattle, WA, April 24, 2012.

11. Anderson, panel presentation at the Association of Theological Schools meeting.

12. Soong-Chan Rah, *The Next Evangelicalism: Releasing the Church from Western Cultural Captivity* (Downers Grove, IL: InterVarsity, 2009), 177; David Kinnaman and Gabe Lyons, *unChristian: What a New Generation Really Thinks about Christianity, and Why It Matters* (Grand Rapids: Baker Books, 2009), 77.

13. Kinnaman and Lyons, *unChristian*, 77–78, 83.

our time are similarly eager to see roots of their social involvement in the actions of those who preceded them. This narrative can again be an impetus for social change, a recovery of the theme for a new generation of evangelicals, and announced with new vigor.

A Rediscovered Evangelicalism for the Twenty-First Century

But should Christians committed to social justice continue to refer to themselves as "evangelicals"? Has the term been so sullied that it no longer has validity? Evangelicalism is often equated with reactionary politics in the public imagination. And because of the negative cast of Christianity in the popular mind as hypocritical and judgmental, some believers now prefer simply to be called "Christ-followers."[14] Has the evangelical label become too much of a lightning rod? Does the evangelical social action that Dayton heralded in 1976 describe a reality for which one may hope, but no longer exists?

Although less visible since 1980, a born-again, justice-minded Christian faith remains a vital force, and can be reclaimed for the sake of the future. Pietistic social reformers continue to be captivated by a call to a transformative religious expression that looks like the nineteenth-century evangelicalism of Finney, Laura Smith Haviland, Samuel Ringgold Ward, Luther Lee, and others. Deep devotion to Christ and to the renewal of the world burgeoned in the nineteenth century and in the 1970s—and can thrive again. The concept of evangelicalism should be retained because an integrated faith that hearkens back to this heritage is more needed than ever. And besides, the alternatives—on the right and on the left—are inadequate for the task.

The orientation of the Religious Right, for instance, does not fit with the inclinations of many twenty-first-century Christians. The Right's nationalistic foreign policy, denial of global warming, reluctance to promote affirmative action or gender equality, legislative restrictions on immigrants, and limitations on government-funded health care do not sit well with most younger Americans. Social scientist Marcia Pally claims that "millions of Christians have left the

14. Ibid.

religious right for anti-consumerist, anti-militarist activism focus-
ing on economic fairness, environmental protection (creation care),
immigration reform, and racial/religious reconciliation." Pally calls
these Christians the "new evangelicals," a term she borrowed from
Richard Cizik, the director of the New Evangelical Partnership for the
Common Good. The new evangelicals of the twenty-first century are
remarkably different from the old post-fundamentalist evangelicals of
the twentieth century; but interestingly, they seem very much like the
even older revivalist evangelicals of the nineteenth century. Indeed,
similar to those written about by Robert Baird in 1844 (and, much
later, by Donald Dayton), the first "core tenet" of the new evangelicalism that Pally describes is "the search for an inner relationship with
Jesus"—an identification based on their experience of regeneration,
not based on a particular doctrinal demarcation or political marker.[15]

The long tradition of evangelicalism, it can be argued, does not
cohere well with rigid dogmatism or far right social views. By contrast, evangelicalism has been most effective when it has identified
with the experiences of the poor and disenfranchised—people on
the edge who (typically) exhibit a profoundly personal encounter
with God. Perhaps the evangelical movement compromises when,
on the one hand, it accommodates to American consumerism or, on
the other hand, participates in cultural disengagement and doctrinal
inflexibility, as it did during the fundamentalist controversy of the
1920s. At that time, conservative Christians overreacted when they
too quickly repudiated the social gospel (which sprang in part from
the social conscience of nineteenth-century evangelicals) along with
their rejection of liberal theology.

But earlier evangelicals did correctly adduce a serious theological
problem when they critiqued certain aspects of late-nineteenth- and
twentieth-century Protestant liberalism. The theological posture of
mainline Christianity, which continues to be manifest in many forms

15. "In-depth Interview with Marcia Pally on *The New Evangelicals*," *Marcia
Pally* website, http://marciapally.com/in-depth-interview-with-marcia-pally-on-the
-new-evangelicals-in-the-art-of-the-good-life/, accessed April 2, 2014; Marcia Pally,
The New Evangelicals: Expanding the Vision of the Common Good (Grand Rapids:
Eerdmans, 2011).

today, is also inadequate for the task of supporting a balanced Christian praxis. In a different way than with conservatism, liberalism is insufficient for an integrated faith and provides yet an additional reason why the message of *evangelical* social activism is pertinent in the twenty-first century.

What is liberalism's inadequacy? Mainline Protestant theology—then and now—minimizes the need for personal conversion and concentrates almost uncritically on human progress, while a more evangelical theology trusts in divine action to bring in God's new creation. Liberal views of progress focus on what happens through the power of this world, while evangelicalism focuses on what comes to this world through the power of the Spirit. The hope for this world does not originate within the world itself, evangelicals declare, but from the Creator who made it and will remake it. Due to their stress on progress, liberals also downplay the inherence and pervasiveness of sin—a problematic theological position that admittedly had a partial genesis in the sermons and writings of Finney and some other nineteenth-century preachers.

To be clear, the large portion of Finney's preaching represented generally accepted Protestant teaching, at least that which is derived from an Arminian perspective. For example, similar to many Christians throughout the history of the church, Finney believed that God's reign could come on earth—that nations can be converted to Christ and that Christ's reign of justice could be effected soon. As Dayton relates (in chap. 10), Finney opposed the Princeton theologians' negative perspective that sinful depravity is the usual human condition and that the power of God's grace to overcome sin is illusory. But Finney's theological orientation went beyond these standard Arminian positions when his preaching tended to verge close to Pelagian works righteousness, especially when he described humanity as having an almost unaided ability to bring about social perfection.

Not all nineteenth-century reformers were as optimistic as Finney about the human condition. At the same time that antebellum evangelical theology lifted up the potential of God's soon-arriving kingdom, many nineteenth-century evangelicals were also "pessimistic about human nature" because of their belief in the persistent likelihood of sin. Most antebellum evangelicals knew the difference between the optimism of American culture (expressed by some religious leaders) and the hopefulness of grace.[16]

This subtle but important theological distinction is evident when we survey the religious history of the post–Civil War era. Liberal Protestants in that period eventually transformed the religious optimism characteristic of Finney into a modernist notion of self-help and an unquestioning acceptance of American global expansionism. Others, however, especially those in the mid- to late-nineteenth-century Holiness and Pentecostal movements, began to have doubts about the inexorable progress of human society. That is, Holiness-oriented evangelicals embraced concepts of human potential early in the nineteenth century, when those concepts coincided with more Arminian views of the expectation of God's grace, but then rejected the trends of religious modernity and liberal progressivism later in the nineteenth century and early in the twentieth century, when those positions were unable or unwilling to be critical of the surrounding culture. The Holiness folk recognized their own continuing proclivity toward evil actions and their complicity in the compromises of bourgeois commercialism and other sinful practices. They knew that they needed God's forgiveness, as provided through the death of Christ, which then led them toward the possibility of being sanctified by grace. Most evangelicals in the nineteenth century thus retained a biblical view of human sin necessary to counteract American hubris and presumption while still confident that the Spirit's power could effect real change in individuals and society. For them, as for contemporary theologian N. T. Wright, "living out a life of Christian holiness makes sense, perfect sense, within God's new world," the world that God is bringing into being by divine initiative, not by human effort alone. Christians in the nineteenth century—and now in the twenty-first century—are drawn to a religious mind-set in which God empowers the transformation of people and the earth's systems. What the created world needs, according to Wright, "is neither abandonment

16. James H. Moorhead, "Social Reform and the Divided Conscience of Antebellum Protestantism," *Church History* 48 (December 1979): 416–30; Leonard I. Sweet, "The View of Man Inherent in New Measures Revivalism," *Church History* 45 (June 1976): 206–21.

[conservative fatalism] nor evolution [liberal concepts of inevitable progress] but rather redemption and renewal."[17]

Along with *theological* liberalism, there are aspects of *political* liberalism that also seem insufficient for today's evangelical ethos. For instance, when some political liberals ridicule and disparage religious piety, it does not help their reputation among Christians. Another example is when political liberals fail to understand why pro-life advocacy is viewed by many Christians as an important cause to be supported along with other life-enhancing policies. The right-to-life issue is especially important within the "consistent life ethic" espoused by a number of evangelicals. Indeed, the incongruity that young Christian voters perceive between their religious convictions and the seemingly inflexible party platforms of either side demonstrates to them that political allegiances are often not as neat as they are purported to be in the reigning polarized partisan discourse.

Contemporary Christians, then, are unconvinced by the prevailing alternatives to a justice-oriented evangelicalism—whether doctrinal exclusiveness and biblical literalism on the one side or mainline Protestant minimization of the effects of sin and the need for conversion on the other; whether conservative fatalism regarding the possibility of social change or liberal accommodation to cultural permissiveness; whether a right-wing political agenda or an entrenched progressive partisanship. For most millennial-generation believers, conservatism seems incapable of addressing the social problems they deem crucial while liberalism seems incapable of addressing the spiritual longings of individuals and communities who recognize their brokenness and need for pardon. Radical evangelicalism, however, offers a tradition and a trajectory that is biblically based, Christ-centered, and socially involved—a gospel that embraces forgiveness and holiness for individuals and redemption and wholeness for the world.

What are the specifics of that trajectory? What portends to be the future of evangelicalism in the United States? These are timely questions because, beginning around the turn of the millennium, the

17. N. T. Wright, *Surprised by Hope: Rethinking Heaven, the Resurrection, and the Mission of the Church* (New York: HarperOne, 2008), 284–85, 107.

membership and attendance of older, primarily white, neo-evangelical churches in the United States started to flatten out and decline, in the same way that the membership of mainline Protestant churches began to decline forty years earlier. Growth still occurs in some predominantly white congregations, but within American evangelicalism as a whole, almost all of the growth appears among the immigrant faith communities of Latino, African, and Asian Americans. The "next Christendom" forecasted by Philip Jenkins—in which Christians from the Global South become preeminent—has become the reality on America's own shores. Rah describes this phenomenon as the "next evangelicalism" of the United States. Majority-culture Christians have the privilege of receiving wisdom from African Americans and those from outside the United States who are now living in America. Perhaps American Christianity as a whole, by tapping into the spiritual vitality of Christians of color, can avoid the growing secularization that has already occurred elsewhere in the West, the religious demise that has contributed to "the death of Christian Britain" and Europe.[18]

Global Christians report on the explosion of God's extraordinary work in their contexts. Americans need to have the humility to be taught by the non-Western church, to be willing to hear from the spirituality of their Christian sisters and brothers from around the world. The next evangelicalism, Rah asserts, has the opportunity to see the African American church and the immigrant church "not as a place of need, but [as] a church community from whom the dominant church could learn." The vital spiritual practices of these communities—such as their early morning prayer and other disciplined prayer customs, their undivided connection between faith and social justice, and especially their conviction that the Holy Spirit is real, active, and present now—can infuse and enliven American Christianity.[19]

In this respect, many younger Christians are finding encouragement in multiethnic congregations popping up all over the United States.

18. Philip Jenkins, *The Next Christendom: The Coming of Global Christianity* (New York: Oxford University Press, 2002); Brian Stanley, *The Global Diffusion of Evangelicalism* (Downers Grove, IL: InterVarsity, 2013); Rah, *The Next Evangelicalism*, 15. See Callum G. Brown, *The Death of Christian Britain* (New York: Routledge, 2001).
19. Rah, *The Next Evangelicalism*, 178.

One such community of believers, Vox Veniae ("voice of forgiveness") in Austin, Texas, found that long-standing "racial lines would not hold" when Christians embraced diverse worship styles and leadership. (This observation about vibrant worship overcoming racial prejudice is reminiscent of the statement by Pentecostal founder Frank Bartleman that "the color line was washed away by the blood" of Jesus at the 1906 Azusa Street revival.) Vox Veniae may be a beacon of the "hope that this kind of postpolitical, postracial congregation is the future of evangelicalism." "In a country that is growing more racially diverse, and in an evangelical movement that is becoming more politically diverse," church groups of this sort represent the aspirations of a large segment of millennial Christianity.[20]

But are theological resources available for the task of cultural engagement and multiethnic ministry required for the next evangelicalism? A robust theological foundation is surely needed. A number of writers and speakers in the past few decades, beginning with Lesslie Newbigin, have articulated a "missional" theology, in which God's apostolic purpose of wholeness and holiness is enacted throughout the world. In answer to the Lord's Prayer, that God's will and God's kingdom will be done on earth as in heaven (Matt. 6:10), missional theologians proclaim that God's love and justice are breaking into this world, resulting in real social change. Through the resurrection of Jesus, God has promised to begin the new creation of individuals and society, characterized by reconciliation at every level of human life. Indeed, the resurrection offers an indication of the direction we should be traveling in—the "future in which death will be done away with and a new creation born." And in light of the dynamism of the resurrection, believers should always be "excelling in the work of the Lord, because you know that in the Lord your labor is not in vain" (1 Cor. 15:58 NRSV). The work of believers here on earth is a signpost of the future that awaits the redeemed in God's eventual new world. According to Wendell Berry, "In the midst of immense problems in this world, rather than despair or cynicism," it is "goodness, beauty,

---

20. Mark Oppenheimer, "Breaking the Evangelical Mold at a Church with Ethnic Roots," *New York Times*, June 7, 2013, http://www.nytimes.com/2013/06/08/us/breaking-the-evangelical-mold-at-an-austin-church.html.

laughter and the summons to get to work to make things better that can give us a sustaining hope."[21] Christians, Wright says, are "the agents of [God's] love going out in new ways, to accomplish new creative tasks, to celebrate and extend the glory of his love." Missional theologians are contending for an "inaugurated eschatology . . . what the resurrection looks like when it comes forward into the moral life of the person of faith."[22] As Jim Wallis wrote in *Post American* magazine in 1972, "Biblical eschatology properly understood is a powerful impulse to social involvement."[23]

In this scripturally informed panorama of God's multicultural new heaven and new earth, men and women of faith are summoned to respond to "the call to conversion": an all-encompassing conversion of personal, Christ-centered change and structural societal change.[24] In the nineteenth century, evangelicals who responded to the call to conversion were on the forefront of social reform—working to end slavery, advocating for the rights of African Americans and other ethnic minorities, encouraging the leadership of women, ministering to the poor, and helping to lessen the harmful systemic effects of alcoholism and consumerism. At several moments in the twentieth century, however, the combination of ardent faith and social action divided. In the twenty-first century, Christians once again have the opportunity to discover how God's vision of the new creation compels people to be change agents, bringing together spiritual fervency with a commitment to participate in God's mission in the world.

---

21. Wendell Berry, interview at American Academy of Religion meeting, Baltimore, MD, November 24, 2013.

22. Wright, *Surprised by Hope*, 104–8, 284–85.

23. Jim Wallis, *Post American* 1, no. 5 (Fall 1972): 2.

24. Jim Wallis, *The Call to Conversion* (New York: Harper & Row, 1981).

Bibliography

Chapter 1. Jonathan Blanchard: The Radical Founder of Wheaton College

Blanchard, Jonathan. *Sermons and Addresses*. Chicago: National Christian Association, 1892.

Blanchard, Jonathan, and N. L. Rice. *A Debate on Slavery*. Cincinnati: Moore, 1846. Reprint, Arno Press of *The New York Times*, Negro History Press, and Negro Universities Press.

Kilby, Clyde. *Minority of One: The Biography of Jonathan Blanchard*. Grand Rapids: Eerdmans, 1959.

Wyeth, Willard W. *Fire on the Prairie: The Story of Wheaton College*. Wheaton: Van Kampen Press, 1950.

Chapter 2. Reform in the Life and Thought of Evangelist Charles G. Finney

Cole, Charles C., Jr. *The Social Ideas of the Northern Evangelists, 1826–1860*. New York: Columbia University Press, 1954.

Finney, Charles G. *Lectures on Revivals of Religion*. Edited by William G. McLoughlin. Cambridge, MA: Belknap Press of Harvard University Press, 1960.

McLoughlin, William G. *Modern Revivalism: Charles G. Finney to Billy Graham*. New York: Ronald Press, 1959.

Rosell, Garth M. "Charles Grandison Finney and the Rise of the Benevolence Empire." PhD diss., University of Minnesota, 1971. Available from University Microfilms, Ann Arbor, MI, order #72–14, 448.

Vulgamore, Melvin L. "Social Reform in the Theology of Charles Grandison Finney." PhD diss., Boston University, 1963. Available from University Microfilms, Ann Arbor, MI, order #64–391.

Chapter 3. Theodore Weld: Evangelical Reformer

Barnes, Gilbert H., and Dwight L. Dumond, eds. *Letters of Theodore Dwight Weld, Angelina Grimké Weld, and Sarah Grimké, 1822–1844.* 2 vols. New York: Appleton-Century, 1934. Reprint, Gloucester, MA: Peter Smith, 1965.

Barnes, Gilbert Hobbs. *The Anti-Slavery Impulse, 1830–1844.* New York: Appleton-Century, 1933. Also available in Harbinger paperback.

Thomas, Benjamin P. *Theodore Weld: Crusader for Freedom.* New Brunswick, NJ: Rutgers University Press, 1950. Reprint, New York: Octagon Press, 1972.

Weld, Theodore. *The Bible Against Slavery.* New York: American Anti-Slavery Society, 1937. Reprint, Detroit: Negro History Press of Detroit, 1970.

———. *Slavery As It Is.* New York: American Anti-Slavery Society, 1839. Reprint, in paperback as *American Slavery As It Is*, Arno Press of the *New York Times*; as *Slavery in America*, ed. Richard Curry and Joanna Dunlap Cowden. Itasca, IL: F. E. Peacock, 1972.

Chapter 4. The Lane Rebellion and the Founding of Oberlin College

Fairchild, James H. *Oberlin: The College and the Colony, 1833–1883.* Oberlin: E. J. Goodrich, 1883.

Fletcher, Robert S. *A History of Oberlin College from Its Foundation through the Civil War.* 2 vols. Oberlin: Oberlin College, 1943. Reprint, Books for Libraries.

Henry, Stuart C. "The Lane Rebels: A Twentieth Century Look." *Journal of Presbyterian History* (Spring 1971): 1–14.

————. *Unvanquished Puritan: A Portrait of Lyman Beecher.* Grand Rapids: Eerdmans, 1973. Chaps. 10 and 11 are on the Lane Rebellion.

Chapter 5. Civil Disobedience and the Oberlin-Wellington Rescue Case

Hosmer, William. *The Higher Law.* Auburn, NY: Derby and Miller, 1852. Reprint, Negro Universities Press, 1969.

Madden, Edward H. *Civil Disobedience and Moral Law in Nineteenth-Century American Philosophy.* Seattle: University of Washington Press, 1968. Also available in a paperback edition.

Shipherd, Jacob R. *History of the Oberlin-Wellington Rescue.* Boston: J. P. Jewett, 1859. Reprint, New York: DaCapo Press, 1972, in their series "Civil Liberties in American History."

Chapter 6. Arthur and Lewis Tappan: The Businessman as Reformer

Abel, Annie Heloise, and Frank J. Klingberg. *A Side-light on Anglo-American Relations 1839–1858.* Washington, DC: The Association for the Study of Negro Life and History, 1927. Reprint, New York: Augustus Kelley, 1970.

Owens, William. *Black Mutiny: The Revolt on the Schooner Amistad.* Philadelphia: Pilgrim Press, 1968.

Tappan, Lewis. *The Life of Arthur Tappan.* New York: Hurd and Houghton, 1870. Reprint, New York: Arno Press of the *New York Times,* 1970.

Wyatt-Brown, Bertram. *Lewis Tappan and the Evangelical War against Slavery.* Cleveland: The Press of Case Western Reserve University, 1969.

Chapter 7. Orange Scott, Luther Lee, and the Wesleyan Methodists

The Autobiography of the Rev. Luther Lee. New York: Phillips and Hunt, 1882.

Dayton, Donald W., ed. *Five Sermons and a Tract by Luther Lee.* Chicago: Holrad House, 1975.

Mathews, Donald G. "Orange Scott: The Methodist Evangelist As Revolutionary." In *The Antislavery Vanguard: New Essays on the Abolitionists.* Edited by Martin Duberman. Princeton: Princeton University Press, 1965.

————. *Slavery and Methodism: A Chapter in American Morality, 1780–1845.* Princeton: Princeton University Press, 1965.

Matlack, L. C. *The Life of the Rev. Orange Scott.* New York: C. Prindle and L. C. Matlack, 1847. Reprinted by Books for Libraries, 1971.

Scott, Orange. *The Grounds of Secession from the M. E. Church.* New York: C. Prindle, 1848. Reprint, New York: Arno Press of the *New York Times*, 1969.

Chapter 8. The Evangelical Roots of Feminism

Dayton, Lucille Sider, and Donald W. Dayton. "'Your Daughters Shall Prophesy': Feminism in the Holiness Movement." *Methodist History* (January 1976): 67–92.

Gordon, A. J. "The Ministry of Women." Gordon-Conwell Monograph no. 61 with an introduction by Pamela Cole. A sixteen-page mimeograph reprint from *Missionary Review of the World* (December 1894): 910–21.

Kraditor, Aileen S. *Up from the Pedestal: Selected Writings in the History of American Feminism.* Chicago: Quadrangle Books, 1968. Also available in paperback.

Lerner, Gerda. *The Grimké Sisters from South Carolina: Pioneers for Women's Rights and Abolition.* New York: Houghton Mifflin, 1967.

Olson, Della E. "A Woman of Her Times." A series of six essays in *The Evangelical Beacon*, May 27, 1975–September 2, 1975.

Roberts, B. T. *Ordaining Women.* Rochester, NY: Earnest Christian Publishing House, 1891.

Rossi, Alice. *The Feminist Papers.* New York: Columbia University Press, 1973. Also available in Bantam paperback.

Starr, Lee Anna. *The Bible Status of Women.* New York: Fleming Revell, 1926. Reprint, Zarephath, NJ: Pillar of Fire, 1955.

Chapter 9. Anointed to Preach the Gospel to the Poor

Booth, William. *In Darkest England and the Way Out.* London: International Headquarters of the Salvation Army, 1890.

Brickley, Donald P. *Man of the Morning: The Life and Work of Phineas F. Bresee.* Kansas City, MO: Nazarene Publishing House, 1960.

Cole, Charles C., Jr. "The Free Church Movement in New York City." *New York History* (July 1953): 284–97.

Heasman, Kathleen. *Evangelicals in Action: An Appraisal of Their Social Work in the Victorian Era.* London: Geoffrey Bles, 1962.

Magnuson, Norris. "Salvation in the Slums: Evangelical Welfare Work, 1865–1920." PhD diss., University of Minnesota, 1968. Available from University Microfilms, Ann Arbor, MI, order #69-1548.

Roberts, B. T. *Pungent Truths.* Chicago: Free Methodist Publishing House, 1912. Reprint, Salem, OH: H. E. Schmul, 1973.

Stead, William T. *If Christ Came to Chicago.* Chicago: Laird & Lee, 1894.

Chapter 10. Whatever Happened to Evangelicalism?

Barker, William S. "The Social Views of Charles Hodge (1797–1878): A Study in 19th-Century Calvinism and Conservatism." *Presbyterion* (Spring 1975): 1–22.

Elliott, E. N., ed. *Cotton Is King, and Pro-Slavery Arguments.* Augusta, GA: Pritchard, Abbott & Loomis, 1860. Reprint, New York: Johnson Reprint Corporation, 1968.

Hogeland, Ronald W. "Charles Hodge, the Association of Gentlemen and Ornamental Womanhood: A Study of Male Conventional Wisdom, 1825–1855." *Journal of Presbyterian History* (Fall 1975): 239–55.

Moberg, David. *The Great Reversal: Evangelism versus Social Concern.* Philadelphia: J. B. Lippincott Company, 1972.

Sandeen, Ernest R. *The Roots of Fundamentalism: British and American Millenarianism, 1800–1930.* Chicago: University of Chicago Press, 1970.